Make-up Designory's
Beauty Make-up

Written by:
Yvonne Hawker

Illustrations by:
Tracie Finite and Ray Santoleri

First Printing 2004

ISBN 0-9749500-1-7

LCCN 2004091104

Trademarked or copyrighted names appearing within:
Barbicide, Japonesque, Mar-Vi-Cide, Polaroid, Webster and Zip-Lock.

Attention Corporations, Universities, Colleges, and Professional Organizations: Quantity discounts are available on bulk purchases of this book for educational or gift purposes. For information, please contact Make-up Designory, 129 S. San Fernando Boulevard, Burbank, CA 91502; ph 818-729-9420.

TABLE OF CONTENTS

Acknowledgements

When Tate Holland first approached me about writing this book, I thought about what a great experience this could be. It has truly been an amazing journey for me, both professionally and personally. This journey, like so many others, is not experienced alone.

First, I wish to express my deepest appreciation and gratitude to John Bailey, whose original beauty artistry program was the basis for this book, and continues to be the heart of the beauty artistry program at Make-up Designory today. Without John's teaching and guidance this book would not have come to fruition. Thank you John!

My sincere appreciation to Michelle Bouse, Michele Davis, Pamela Hackeman, T.C. Luisi, Ashlee Petersen, Lisa Ruckh, Paul Thompson and Mary Anne Toccalino. Collectively, their knowledge and experience as Make-up Designory faculty and staff members have contributed in many ways to the outcome of this book. It has been a pleasure to work with all of them!

In addition, I wish to acknowledge the other individuals who have also been a part of this amazing process. Derek Althen, whose wonderful photographs have brought such clarity and life to the tools of our trade. To Tracie Finite for being able to translate my visions into beautiful illustrations, thank you for your talent and expertise. Ray Santoleri, whose illustrations are still greatly appreciated and used on a daily basis in our classrooms. Peter Lambertz, for all the long hours of making sure everything was just right, and whose insight was invaluable. And to Patricia Holland and Julie Reich for their editorial suggestions, which showed remarkable depth of knowledge.

Also, my sincere appreciation to all of the people who have guided, helped out, or had suggestions in making this book a reality. Special heartfelt thanks to Tate Holland for giving me the opportunity to write this book and grow through the experience.

Yvonne Hawker
Instructor
Make-up Designory

PREFACE

This book is the result of the collaborative work, expertise, and individual strengths of the Make-up Designory instructors. Our goal is to provide the reader with a well-rounded view of the fundamentals of beauty artistry. While written for the beginning student, the information presented may serve as a reference for the student and the working professional.

Beauty Make-Up is an art form onto itself that uniquely combines creativity with technical skills. As in all art forms, it is essential that the artist also be familiar with the principles and fundamentals needed in the craft of make-up artistry. Once the make-up artist knows these principles and fundamentals, creativity can flourish.

Accordingly, this book has been written to allow you to build your skills in small increments while increasing confidence with hands-on practice. Reading alone will not make you an artist. Dedication to the craft and hours of practice are required in order to become a proficient make-up artist. Practice the exercises in the book repeatedly. Feel free to experiment with different types of products and textures and do not limit yourself by working on one type of face or skin tone. Diversity of models and products will allow you to develop your skill and your artistic style.

Being a make-up artist can be such a rewarding, fulfilling profession with truly endless possibilities. Make-Up artists work in film, television, print, retail, salons and even with plastic surgeons and cancer patients. Whatever your chosen area might be, it is important that you make it your first goal to become proficient with the fundamentals of the craft. It is our goal and hope that this book brings you closer to fulfilling your own goals.

Enjoy

CHAPTER 1

A BRIEF HISTORY OF MAKE-UP——

EGYPTIANS-4,000 BC

Evidence shows that the Egyptians were amongst the first to use cosmetics, painting their eyebrows, as well as outlining their eyes with a heavy application of kohl. (Kohl was a cream made from the fat of sheep mixed with powdered lead or antimony and soot.) They also used a bright green paste made from copper minerals to paint their faces, in order to protect them from the hot Egyptian sun. The ancient Egyptians were also amongst the first to enjoy a bath rich in milk and honey to soften the skin.

THE FAR EAST-1500 BC

In ancient China and Japan, faces were painted white with a rice-powder paint, eyebrows were plucked and teeth painted black or gold. Henna dyes were used to stain hair and faces. (Henna has been used in many cultures for approximately 5,000 years, and is still in use today.) Made from the bush *Lawsonia incermis*, the plant is dried and crushed into a fine powder. In its powdered state it is dark green; however, it stains as orange-red.

ROMANS AND GREEKS-100 AD

The Romans used wine to stain their cheeks and painted their faces and arms with chalk to get that pallid look. They used crocodile excrement for mud baths, barley flour and butter for pimples, and sheep fat and blood for nail polish. Men and women frequently dyed their hair blonde, but the dyes containing lye were so caustic that many people lost their hair and had to wear wigs. The Greeks used vermillion for rouge, as well as the juice from berries to stain their cheeks and lips. Black incense was used to darken the lashes.

THE MIDDLE AGES

This was a time when women were so desperate to be pale that they allowed themselves to be bled or painted. Tattooing was also popular during this time. Eye shadow was used in varying colors of green, blue, gray and brown.

14th CENTURY

This was the time of the Black Plague, when cosmetics were thought of as a threat. Thinking they might interfere with energy circulating properly, people chose other means to decorate their bodies.

In Elizabethan England, faces were painted with white lead or powdered borax, and wigs dyed red were in fashion. Ochre and mercuricsulphide were used for cheek rouge. Lips were painted with egg whites and fig milk mixed with cochineal. (Egg whites were also used to "glaze" the skin.)

15th-16th CENTURIES

Used only by royalty, their courtiers, and the aristocracy, cosmetics reappeared in Europe, manufactured primarily in Italy and France. France was busy creating new fragrances (perfume) by blending multitudes of ingredients, including, plants and flowers.

Whitening agents for the face were used, composed of carbonate, hydroxide, and lead oxide. These agents cumulatively stored in the body with each use and were responsible for numerous physical problems which resulted in some cases in muscle paralysis or death. The damage inflicted by the lead was unintentional but the use of arsenic face powder was not.

17th-18th CENTURIES

Cosmetics were in use by nearly all social classes. Liquid arsenic was used to make the skin pale; however, this caused a shedding reaction resulting in women losing their skin. Red rouge and lipstick were the rage, implying a healthy, fun-loving spirit. Other countries felt the French must have something to hide as they were repulsed by the excessive use of make-up in France.

19th CENTURY

Early in the 1800's make-up became less theater-like and swung to the more subtle and natural application. France developed and manufactured new chemical processes, replacing the natural methods. Zinc oxide became widely used as a facial powder, and is still in use today. Zinc oxide took the place of the deadly arsenic mixture. Eye shadows and lip reddeners contained poisonous substances such as lead, antimony sulfide, and mercuric sulfide. Belladonna, or deadly nightshade, was used to make one's eyes sparkle. It was a deadly poison when used in large amounts.

20th CENTURY-EARLY 1900s

The turn of the century saw the commercial cosmetics industry find its earliest substantial growth. Handbags sold to ladies of this period were generally stocked with cosmetic accessories, such as powder puffs and rouge. Lipstick was first manufactured in the United States, and Helena Rubinstein developed a line of cosmetics, including the first mascara. Theda Bara, an American actress of the silent-film era (Cleopatra, Salome), caused a sensation when she appeared on the screen heavily adorned with Helena Rubinstein's cosmetics. Borrowing the idea of color-shaded eyes from the French stage, Helena also developed colored eye powders.

1920s

Women of the twenties were in a period of self discovery. They shed their long locks, painted their faces and wore clothing that exposed their arms and legs. Kohl reappeared, and women once again rimmed their eyes. Eyebrows were worn dark and overextended. Lips were bright red in the now famous "bee-stung" shape. Towards the end of the 20's mascara appeared and women wore it proudly, showing off their thick black lashes.

1930s

Unlike make-up of the twenties, the make-up of the thirties was intended to show off the beauty of the face rather than disguise it. It was all about the image, a means of escape from the overwhelming sadness of the depression. More cosmetics were used, creating a look of less. Sculptured was the word used to describe the polished look of the thirties.

1940s

With the war came a shortage of everything, including make-up. Advertisers asked women to save their make-up for the evenings, and women listened. During the day, they cleansed, moisturized and powdered their faces, and even lipstick was saved for evening nights out. False eye lashes became popular in Hollywood and, for the first time, women wore make-up on their legs instead of stockings, using a pancake make-up over the entire leg with an eyebrow pencil drawing, in a seam, down the back of the leg.

1950s

With the war behind them and an economy of growth, women took on a traditional look of elegance, (lips and eyes were major points of cosmetic emphasis.) With heavily applied foundation, thinly lined eyes, well manicured brows and beautifully applied red lipstick, women became classy.

1960s

No longer a classic look, make-up during the sixties took on more of a free-spirit attitude with lips painted white or purple, and Egyptian-style eyeliner, to fantasy images, such as butterflies painted on the face. Both false eyelashes and natural cosmetic products, or those based on botanical ingredients, grew in popularity.

1970s

This was a time when women could change their make-up from one extreme to the next, all within the same day, natural and fresh while at work, heavy and colorful when stepping out in the evening. Iridescent shadows and lip gloss arrived on the market, and women couldn't get enough of them.

1980s

Music video was introduced, giving cosmetic companies a new market in which to promote their product. The heavy eyeliner look remained in style, with wide color ranges available for decorating the lids of women and men alike. Not so natural colors like pink, purple and orange could be seen on faces and in hair.

1990s

This decade brought a wide array of looks, from clean and natural to bright colors and glitter. A popular look early in the nineties would have been dark eyes with light lips. Another look for lips would be rimming the lips with dark lip liner followed by lips filled in with a light gloss. New cosmetic companies popped up yearly, catering to the very young consumer as well as the mature one.

2000+

Today, the American cosmetics and beauty-aid industry totals over $20 billion in annual sales, and is dominated by hair and skin-care products that are heavily advertised in print and on television. Bright colors, or the natural look, can be found in every magazine all over the world. More fashion magazines are in print than ever before, which has a profound effect on how women of this century view themselves and how they look.

CHAPTER STUDY QUESTIONS

1. Where were faces believed to be painted with rice?

2. What material was used to paint ancient Egyptian eyebrows?

3. What product did the ancient Romans color their cheeks with?

4. What material was used as a base in Elizabethan England?

5. What was used to glaze the skin in Elizabethan England?

6. What material did the ancient Romans use to paint their faces and arms?

7. In the middles ages what technique did women use to keep themselves pale?

8. When did zinc oxide emerge as a cosmetic?

9. When did women start to use make-up on their legs?

10. Who developed the first mascara?

CHAPTER 2

SANITATION

As a make-up artist, sanitation is a very important part of maintaining a clean and professional environment. Good practices will keep your tools and materials contaminant free. The cleanliness of you and your station is the first step in conveying competence to the individuals you will be working on.

BASIC SANITATION PRACTICES

YOU

Maintain a clean and neat appearance with appropriate attire for the job. A waterless hand sanitizer must be at your station and in your set bag at all times and should be used in between each person. After eating or smoking, wash your hands with soap and water, sanitize them and consider brushing your teeth. Have mints or breath spray handy at all times.

TOOLS

All brushes should be cleaned with a professional grade of brush cleaner after each use. Be sure to use a brush cleaner designed only for make-up brushes. Do not wait until you have another individual to work on as the brushes need to be thoroughly dry before each use. Clean and used brushes should be kept separate.

Palettes and palette knives may be sanitized with 99% alcohol after each use. 99% alcohol in a spray bottle works well in this application.

Sponges and puffs should be used on **ONE** person only and thrown out after every use. They are disposable and should be treated as such. You may choose to maintain a sponge or a puff inside a Zip-Lock bag for a single individual. This is acceptable providing that it is thrown out at the end of the day. It is not acceptable to use either of these tools on multiple persons. When maintaining a sponge or puff in this manner it is recommended that the bag be clearly identified with the individual's name.

Disposable mascara wands are just that, and should not be returned to a mascara container after they have touched any part of the face. To avoid having to use multiple mascara wands the mascara may be removed from the container and placed on a palette. You may also assign a container/tube of mascara to each individual, clearly identified with their name.

Combs and hair brushes need to be chemically sanitized with a state-approved disinfectant such as Barbicide or Mar-Vi-Cide. These chemicals come in a concentrated form and need to be diluted with water. It is recommended that the make-up artist follow the manufacturer's directions listed on the containers for formulas and working times.

Once a comb or brush has been used on an individual or has fallen to the floor, it is no longer sanitary and needs to be sanitized before it may be used again.

Clean combs and brushes need to be kept separate from used combs and brushes. It is recommended that the make-up artist have containers clearly marked, indicating which combs and brushes are clean and which have been used.

PRODUCT

There are several things that should be done to ensure the sanitation and safety of the individuals you will be working on.

First, do not "double-dip". This means not working out of the containers. Palette knives may be used to remove small amounts of product to be placed on a palette. The make-up artist will work from the palette, not the container.

This is most important when working with cream products such as base, mascara and lipstick.

Although not quite as critical, powder products may be sanitized by the use of 99% alcohol in a spray form. A light mist is sufficient to maintain sanitary practices. Do not soak your powder products with alcohol as this will compact then crack the product.

When using lip or eye pencils it is important to sharpen them just before use and to spray them with 99% alcohol. The pencil sharpener should also be sprayed with 99% alcohol to maintain sanitary practices.

Bacteria grows primarily in moist, warm areas. Do not leave your make-up kit in the car. When not in use store your make-up kit in a cool place. Liquid make-up may be stored in the refrigerator to avoid separation.

All make-up has a shelf life. If at any time it develops an undesirable odor it would be advisable to replace it. Shelf life can vary greatly, with liquid and creams having the shortest duration; powders may last a long time.

TIPS

While working it is good practice to use a puff with the powdered side toward the face. This will keep the make-up from transferring to your hand.

Do not blow on your make-up brushes or tap them on the chair.

Placing tissue around the collar or cover cloth will prevent make-up from rubbing off onto the clothing.

A small paper trash bag taped to the counter of your station will help to keep your station clean.

When setting up your station use a sanitary placemat. When it becomes dirty it is easily replaced.

Keep your kit clean and organized.

CHAPTER STUDY QUESTIONS

1. When should you use hand sanitizer?

2. What is a way to convey confidence to a performer?

3. When should brushes be cleaned?

4. Can a sponge be used multiple times if sanitized with 99% alcohol?

5. How is a palette sanitized?

6. Where does bacteria primarily grow?

7. Shoud disposable mascara wands be dipped more than once in the container?

8. Are Barbicide and Mar-vi-cide state approved products to sanitize?

9. When is it necessary to throw away a puff?

10. When using a cream product is it acceptable to work directly from the container?

CHAPTER 3

BASE ─────────────────────────────

The base application process is the first step in doing a beauty make-up. The following concepts will be addressed in this chapter: Proper application of base for an even, consistent coverage, color that matches or enhances the appearance of the skin, coverage with reduction or neutralization of minor skin discoloration.

After completing this chapter, the artist will be able to apply a consistent surface for the effective application of the decorative elements of the make-up.

ELEMENTS OF BASE

There are two elements that determine the color, coverage and application of the base. These two elements are **Vehicle** and **Pigment**.

Vehicle is the element of the base that gives it its slip, or the ability to move on the face during application. The easier a base moves on the face, the lighter the slip. The more drag a base has, the stiffer the "slip".

Pigment is the element of the base that provides shade/color and coverage. The less pigment a base contains, the less coverage it will deliver.

The base will also have a light slip. This type of base will be sheer in its application.

The greater the amount of pigment, the more coverage a base will deliver. The base will also have a stiffer slip. This type of base will be more dense in its application.

BASE AND SKIN CARE

Before considering which types of base will work best for each individual, the condition of the skin must be evaluated.

Skin that is in good shape will generally have an even surface, making for a smoother, overall application of base.

Skin that is in need of attention, such as dry skin, will be more likely to have an uneven application of base and may possibly have areas on the skin that are uneven in color as a result.

Skin that tends to be oily will also need attention, so first remove the oily residue. If this is not done prior to the application of the base the excessive oil on the skin, combined with the base, will not allow the base to adhere to the skin.

A regimented routine of cleansing, moisturizing and exfoliating will help to maintain the skin in a healthy state. Use a professional line of skin care products, appropriate for the model's skin type, to cleanse the face. A word of caution in regard to exfoliating: Skin that is over-exfoliated can be a problem as well. If the surface is too smooth, base may not stay on the skin.

Choosing a base with SPF 15 will help to maintain the skin in a healthy condition, protecting it from the negative effects of the sun.

TYPES OF BASE

There are three primary types of base: **Cream, Liquid, Dual Finish**.

CREAM:

The choice for maximum coverage. This type of base is a popular choice for film, video and still photography.

Uses cream as a vehicle and contains a high concentration of pigment. This type of base works well to even out skin tones. This base has the most versatility as it can be used "as is" for a concentrated coverage or it may be sheered out by adding a cream moisturizer.

LIQUID:

Is a popular choice for a light or sheer coverage. It is easy to use, and has a light slip. This base may also be used as body make-up.

DUAL FINISH:

May include pressed powders. This product combines some of the elements of a cream base (coverage) with the matte effects of a powder.

It is easy to use and contains no vehicle, so talc is used to add slip. It may be applied with a sponge, puff or brush. For a sheer application or if stronger coverage is required, it may be applied wet or dry.

SHADE AND UNDERTONE

This lesson is designed to give the make-up artist an understanding of the variety and subtlety of the shades found in bases, and in human skin. The make-up artist will also learn to apply this information when conducting a base skin tone match. **Shade** and **Undertone** are the two visual elements necessary for an accurate base skin tone match.

Shade is the lightness or darkness of a base. Shade can be visualized by use of the **Gray Scale.**

"**0**" equals white, "**10**" equals black, and everything in between is a shade, at even increments of 10%. In other words, each shade is 10% darker than the one before it. White is 0%, with black being 100%.

The shade of every base can be found somewhere on the Gray Scale. The shade of every human face will also be found on the Gray Scale. Remember that it is not that a shade is gray in color but rather gray represents the lightness to darkness of that shade.

GRAY SCALE

This illustration shows the Lightness to Darkness of the **Gray Scale.**
Each box is 10% darker than the one before it.

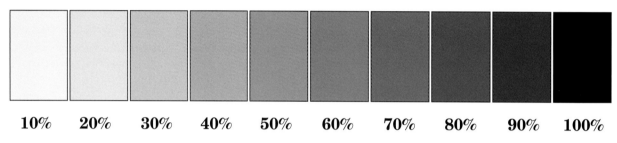

| 10% | 20% | 30% | 40% | 50% | 60% | 70% | 80% | 90% | 100% |

SHADE

EXERCISE

Using a cream product series, arrange the bases in ascending order, from light to dark, the lightest shade on the left, and the darkest on the right. All base series have obvious and subtle differences in shade.

When arranging bases, there will be times when the differences are not clear. After identifying the shades of the bases, use the base **Gray Scale** worksheet to record the results.

Remove a small amount of base from the container with a make-up palette knife and place it in the designated circles on the worksheet in ascending order, from light to dark. By following this procedure the shade differences become more apparent. Fill in the labels over each base, with the name or number of each color.

NOTE:

After removing the product with a palette knife, be sure to wipe the palette knife clean before moving to the next shade. This will ensure that the color does not contaminate the previous shade, and will give a true reading of the colors.

UNDERTONE

The second visual element necessary for a successful skin tone match is called **Undertone.** Undertone is the intrinsic color of the skin. The skin color of some people is rich in undertone, and can be seen easily, while the undertone in others is more obscure.

Undertone color can range from ruddy (pink to reddish) to olive (yellow-green to green-yellow) and may include blue. Therefore, base colors are produced in a variety of skin undertones, ranging from ruddy to olive. The greatest majority of undertones are olive.

Undertone colors can vary from series to series, from product line to product line with some series having very little undertone, while others will be rich in undertone. By arranging the bases in order of most ruddy to least ruddy, and from most olive to least olive, the make-up artist will be able to see that some of the differences will be obvious while others can be subtle.

To effectively see these subtle differences, good lighting is essential. When working with base application, make sure that the work area is well-lit. To further enhance the ability to see the undertone, apply small amounts of the bases, side-by-side, on white paper. This will aid in distinguishing colors by providing a neutral background. Also, a white cover cloth on the model is suggested during the make-up application. White will give a true reading of the model's skin tone, which is necessary for base matching. A colored cover cloth will reflect that color on the model's skin, making it impossible to accurately see or match the skin's undertone.

EXERCISE

Using a cream product series, arrange the Bases in ascending order, "from ruddy" to olive. The least amount of ruddy on the left, to the most amount of olive on the right.

After identifying the undertones of the bases, use the base Ruddy to Olive worksheet to record the results. Remove a small amount of base from the bottle with a palette knife and place it in the designated circles on the worksheet in ascending order.

By following this procedure, the undertone differences become more apparent. Fill in the labels above each base, with the name or number of each color. Be sure to wipe the make-up palette knife clean between colors so you do not contaminate or mix colors. In this exercise shade makes no difference; you are searching for the undertones only.

NOTE:

Keep in mind that shade is different than undertone. When arranging the undertones, the order may be very different than when placing the order of the shades.

MATCHING SKIN TONE

Becoming more aware of the shade in base and skin is the first step in developing a discerning eye for base and skin tone matching. Observe the overall skin shade of people. Is the face lighter or darker than the neck, arms or legs? Notice that not everyone's face is all one color. There may be subtle or major differences in the color of a person's face. Consider where to place them on the Gray Scale. Observe the undertone color. Are they ruddy or olive? How much ruddiness is there? How much olive is there? Matching skin tones is a combination of both shade (light to dark) and undertone (ruddy to olive). Remember, the majority of the world's population has some amount of olive undertone in the skin . When observing the true undertone of the skin, one may become distracted by the variety of shade colors in the face. Which one of the colors in the face should be matched?

When examining the color of the skin one may find redness caused by blemishes, irritation, blood vessels, or blueness around the eyes or veins close to the surface of the skin. These colors are distractions that may divert the artist's attention from the true undertone color of the skin.

The face may also have subtle differences of the shade and undertone from one facial area to another. Notice that there may be a strong difference between the face and neck, especially if one wears base with a sunscreen. (In the summer this may become quite noticeable. A good base match will reduce or eliminate this problem.) For the majority of people, the most effective area for an accurate skin match is just below and in front of the ear. In this location, the undertone is more clear. The neck joins the face in this area, allowing the artist to see the undertone and the shade of the face and neck.

EXERCISE

To gain an understanding of how to match different bases or combinations of bases and how that relates to shade and undertone, look at the differences in color between the outside of the forearm and the inside of the forearm. Generally, the outside will be darker than the inside.

In a well-lit area, observe the differences. These differences occur primarily from the amount of exposure to the sun. Using a cream base, select a base color that appears to be the closest in shade and undertone to the outside of the forearm. If no "one" base gives a perfect match, then try to mix, or combine, the two closest matches.

SHADE:

When the base is too light or too dark on the skin: Too light – add a small amount of a darker base, and mix together. This can be done by using the palette knife and the palette to mix the products together. Continue adding small amounts until the desired shade is reached. Too dark – add a small amount of a lighter base, and mix together. Continue adding small amounts until the desired shade is reached.

UNDERTONE:

If no one base gives a perfect match, then mix, or combine the two closest base matches. When one base is slightly light and a little too ruddy and another base is slightly dark and a little too olive, mix these two bases together. The make-up artist will produce the correct color combination. When mixing colors, use a palette. Now, apply a small amount of base, using a make-up sponge, to the outside of the forearm. Continue choosing/mixing colors, until there is an accurate match.

When the base color and shade disappear on the skin, this is a perfect skin tone match. The desired objective is for the base to be undetectable, and natural. Once this match is completed, choose a base color to match the inside of the forearm, and repeat the above process.

BASE APPLICATION

Applying base to the face using one of the three different types of base (cream, liquid, or dual finish) may require different methods and/or tools.

When applying any of these bases, it is important to use the products in moderation. This way the artist will have control over the quality of the finished look.

It is much easier to add product, if needed, rather than having too much on the face and having to remove it. Too much product will result in streaking, leaving the application uneven.

Using the previously discussed techniques for matching bases, the artist is ready to begin the applicational techniques.

CREAM BASE APPLICATION

EXERCISE

Before beginning with the application process, be sure your station is clean and organized. Arrange all the products and tools you will need. When working with a cream base an application using a make-up sponge will yield the best results. The sponge will aid in providing a streak-free, even coverage.

Match the base to the model's skin tone, referring to that section in this chapter. Always work from the palette, not the container of base. It is considered very unsanitary to dip the sponge into the make-up container as this may contaminate the make-up, making it unusable for any other person.

LOADING THE SPONGE

Once the matched base is on the palette, the artist is ready for the next step, loading the sponge. To do so, follow these steps.

• Hold the sponge between the thumb and middle finger. Place the index finger behind the sponge, at the application point. Gently pat the sponge on the base, until a complete, even coverage is achieved on the application area of the sponge. This is generally along the top of the wedge portion of the sponge.

• Avoid building up excessive amounts of base on the sponge. This happens when the surface area of the sponge has been loaded to the point that the surface texture of the sponge has been hidden by the build up of base. Too much base on the sponge will produce a base application that appears heavy. Also, streaking will occur. If too much base is loaded on the sponge, the excess may be removed by tapping the excess on the back of the hand, or blotting with a tissue.

APPLICATION

Once the sponge has been loaded properly, apply the base by pressing the sponge gently on the face.

• One method is to use a short stroking motion. Another method is to roll the sponge gently from side to side while going over the surface of the skin. Using either method takes practice in order to develop a consistent application process, increasing your speed and creating an even coverage.

• One process which works well is to begin with the forehead, working down one side of the face, blending the base. Then past the jaw-line and onto the neck to avoid leaving a distinguishable line of base that might leave a mask effect. Leave the eye area for last. Repeat the process for the other side.

• During the application process, continually load small amounts of base on the sponge. By doing this you avoid a heavy build up in any one area

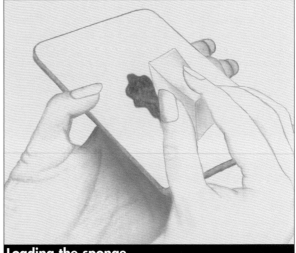

Loading the sponge

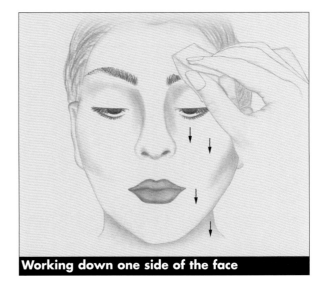

Working down one side of the face

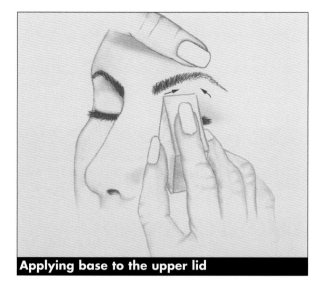

Applying base to the upper lid

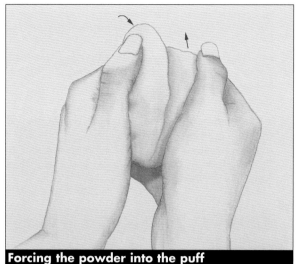

Forcing the powder into the puff

• Gently apply base under the eye all the way to the lash line. When applying base around the eyes, it is important not to pull, tug or drag the sponge across this sensitive tissue. A gentle rolling motion works well in these delicate areas. The base should be applied lightly over the upper lid. It is important to apply base to the lid area, not only to correct color problems but also to provide a clean, smooth and consistent surface for the application of eye shadows and liner. If this is not done, the eye shadow will not adhere well to the dry areas, and will build up excessively on the oily areas. The eye area requires very little product. It is a good idea to ask the model if she is wearing contact lenses. If this is the case the make-up artist will need to proceed with caution, being sure not to apply excess pressure to the eyelid area.

• To apply base to the upper lid, first have the model close her eyes, then place the thumb over the eyebrow, and gently lift so as to tighten the upper lid. If this is not done, the skin of the upper lid will move with the sponge, and the base will not transfer from the sponge to the lid.

• With the sponge, gently apply base on the brow bone, just below the eyebrow. Move down the lid, to the lash line. It is necessary to apply base to the lash line so that a consistent eyeliner application may be achieved.

• Check the base application for even coverage, adding more where necessary, and blending any areas with excessive build up.

• After the base application has been completed, powder is applied to "set" the make-up. If this is not done, the base will smear and rub off easily. To set the base, use loose powder and a powder puff.

Rolling the puff to apply powder

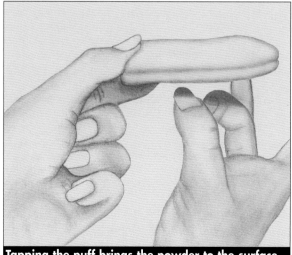

Tapping the puff brings the powder to the surface

LOADING THE PUFF

• To load the puff, apply powder from the center to an edge of the puff. Fold the puff over the powder. Rub both sides together, forcing the powder into the puff. The powder that has been forced into the puff may be brought to the surface by tapping the puff with the finger.

• Several applications of powder may be loaded into the puff at one time. Wrap the puff around the index finger, and apply the powder by pressing and rolling the puff over the base in the same pattern in which the base was applied.

• As more powder is needed, simply tap the underside of the powder puff, bringing more powder to the surface.

• When applying powder to the upper lid area, tighten the lid area in the same manner as for the base application. Use the tip of the finger or the sponge to smooth out any creases that may have developed, placing the corner of the puff on the eye, and roll the puff over the eye. Never pat or press hard over the eye. If the lid is not smooth before powdering, any creases or build up will be "set" in place. The base is now ready for the decorative application.

DUAL FINISH BASE APPLICATION

EXERCISE

Before beginning with the application process, be sure your station is clean and organized. Have out all the items you will need.

The Dual Finish base will deliver a very light to medium light coverage, depending upon the application technique: brush, dry sponge, or damp sponge.

When working with a Dual Finish base, an application using either a make-up sponge or blush brush will produce the best results. These methods will aid in providing a streak-free, even coverage.

• Match the base to the person's skin tone, referring to that section in this chapter. The artist may apply directly from the container, only when this product is personally owned by the make-up artist's model and is not to be shared with any one else. This is to prevent the spread of bacteria. If this is not the case, however, it is suggested that the artist scrape a small amount of product, using a palette knife to place it onto a palette and working from the palette to apply. This will keep the product contaminate free.

BRUSH APPLICATION

• Using a blush brush is a convenient way to apply this powdered base. This brush will deliver a light to very light coverage. For small areas around the eyes and nose the make-up artist may also use an eye shadow or foundation brush.

• To load the brush, apply evenly by working the bristles of the brush gently into the base using a light circular motion. This will ensure that the application area of the brush is evenly covered with base. If this is not done, the base may become too concentrated on one side of the brush, making an even base application inconsistent.

• Working from the forehead down, and with a gentle touch, apply base in a consistent pattern using short, light half-circle strokes with the brush. The base will transfer quickly to the face. Re-load brush as needed.

• Continue down the face, leaving the eyelids for last. Choose to either go down one side then the other, or work horizontally across the face. Developing a consistent pattern in the application process is important. When approaching the neck area, be sure to blend off the base edges.

• The powdered base should be applied lightly to the eyelids, to create an even, smooth and consistent surface for the application of decorative and corrective eye make-up.

• To apply base to the upper eyelid, have the model close her eyes and place your thumb over the eyebrow, at the arch. Gently lift the eyebrow, to tighten the upper lid. This is done to reduce creases in the eyelid, and to prevent the eyelid from moving with the brush.

• Lightly load the blush brush with the dual finish base, gently brushing over the upper eyelid area, beginning on the brow bone and moving towards the lashes. Some eye shapes may prevent a powder brush from reaching the inner corner of the eye. If necessary you may use an eye shadow brush.

• Lightly load the bristles with base, and apply where needed. Gently apply the base with very short strokes under each eye, all the way to the bottom lash line.

• Check the base for an even coverage, adding more where necessary, and blending off areas of excess. The base is now ready for the decorative application.

DRY SPONGE APPLICATION

• The dry sponge will deliver a light to medium light coverage. To load the sponge, hold it between the thumb and middle finger. The index finger should be placed behind the sponge, at the application point.

• Gently press the sponge into the dual finish base, using a circular motion to load the sponge. Excess base build-up might develop on the sponge. This will cause a streaky, uneven base application. To correct this, blot the sponge on a tissue or the back of your hand to even out the base.

• Once the sponge has been loaded properly, gently press the sponge against the face. Use a gentle short stroking motion to avoid streaking and build-up.

• It is necessary to develop a consistent application process to increase your speed and create an even coverage. Do not move around the face; for example, applying first to the left eye, then the forehead, then the neck, then the right eye. This will only slow down the application process and make it difficult to achieve an even coverage. During the application continually load small amounts of base on the sponge as needed.

• It is important to apply base to the eyelid area to provide a clean, smooth surface for the application of eye shadows and eye liner.

• To apply base to the upper eyelid, first lightly load the sponge with base. Have the model close her eyes. Place your thumb on the eyebrow, at the arch point. Gently lift the brow to tighten the upper lid. If this is not done, the skin of the upper lid will move with the sponge and the base will not transfer evenly. With the sponge, gently apply base on the brow bone and work your way down to the lash line.

• Gently apply in small strokes under the eye, all the way to the lash line.

• Check for an even coverage, adding more where necessary and blending off areas with excessive build-up. The base is now ready for the decorative application.

DAMP SPONGE APPLICATION
• The use of water as a vehicle will give a more opaque coverage. For a wet application, it is best to use a sponge.

• The sponge should be damp. Wet the entire sponge with water. Squeeze, holding the sponge between the thumb and middle finger. The index finger should be placed behind the sponge at the application point.

• Place the sponge on the base, using a circular stroking motion to work the base evenly into the sponge. If the base is streaky, or uneven, the base may contain too much moisture. Remove the excess moisture by squeezing the sponge, and begin the loading process again.

• If the base accumulates in small clumps and/or feels thick or pasty, then there is too little moisture. Add a small amount of water to the sponge and repeat the loading process. There should be just enough moisture to make the base light and smooth. After a few applications the amount of moisture necessary will be easy to judge.

• Once the sponge has been loaded properly, apply the base by pressing the sponge gently on the face. Use a short stroking motion to avoid streaking and build-up. It is necessary to develop a consistent application process to increase your speed and create an even coverage. For example: Begin with the forehead, then work down one side of the face, then down the other side of the face, blending off the base past the jaw-line and onto the neck.

• During the application process, continually load small amounts of base on the sponge. This is done to ensure a consistent coverage.

• Gently apply base under the eye, all the way to the lower lash line. It is important to apply base to the upper eyelid area, to correct color problems and provide a smooth and consistent surface for the application of the eye shadow and eye liner.

• To apply base to the upper eyelid, have the model close her eyes, place your thumb over the eyebrow and gently lift the brow, to tighten the upper eyelid. This will make the transfer of make-up to the lid much easier.

• With the sponge, gently apply base to the brow bone, just below the eyebrow. Move down the lid, all the way to the lash line.

• Check the base for an even coverage, and adjust wherever necessary.

LIQUID BASE APPLICATION

EXERCISE
Before beginning with the application process, be sure your station is clean and organized. Have out all the items you will need.
Liquid base generally will produce the lightest of coverage and may be applied with either a wet sponge or dry sponge application.

WET SPONGE APPLICATION
Liquid base application with a wet sponge will produce a very light, even coverage. The base's liquid is not absorbed by the sponge because of the water content in the sponge, keeping the base's coverage sheer.

LOADING THE SPONGE

• Wet the sponge and squeeze out any excess moisture. The sponge should only be damp; water should not drip from the sponge. Hold the sponge between the thumb and middle finger, with the index finger placed behind the sponge at the application point.

• A small amount of base may be placed on a palette or the back of the hand. Gently pat the sponge on the base until a complete coverage is achieved.

APPLICATION

• Once the sponge has been loaded, apply the base by pressing the sponge gently on the face. Use a short stroking motion for consistent coverage. Develop a consistent application process to increase your speed and complete coverage.

• During the application process continually load small amounts of base on the sponge.

• Make sure to apply under the eyes to the lashes. Apply base to the upper eyelid by having the model close her eyes. Placing the thumb over the eyebrow, gently lift to tighten the upper eyelid.

• With the sponge, gently apply base on the brow bone, just below the eyebrow, using very short and light strokes, all the way down the eyelid to the lash line.

• Check the base for even coverage, adding more where necessary and blending off areas with excessive build-up.

DRY SPONGE APPLICATION

• Liquid base, applied with a dry sponge, will produce a light to very light presentation.

• When using a dry sponge, the base is absorbed by the sponge. This will slightly increase the coverage of the liquid.

LOADING THE SPONGE

• Hold the sponge between the thumb and middle finger. The index finger should be placed behind the sponge, at the application point. A small amount of the base may be placed on a palette or back of the hand.

• Gently pat the sponge on the base until a complete, even coverage is achieved.

APPLICATION

• Once the sponge has been loaded, apply the base by pressing the sponge gently on the face. Use a short stroking motion for consistent coverage. Develop a consistent application process to increase your speed and efficiency.

• During the application process, continually load small amounts of base on the sponge.

• Make sure to apply base under the eyes, all the way to the lashes. Apply base to the upper eyelid by having the model close her eyes. Place your index finger over the eyebrow, and gently lift so as to tighten the upper eyelid.

• With the sponge, gently apply base on the brow bone, just below the eyebrow, using very short and light strokes, all the way down on the eyelid to the lash line.

• Check the base for even coverage, adding more where necessary, and blending off areas with excessive build-up.

• Always check the match in the mirror. This will give a much truer reading of the make-up application. Checking in this manner allows the artist to view the application as the camera will read it.

CHAPTER STUDY QUESTIONS

1. What elements are involved in matching skin tones?

2. Is skin care an important factor in base application?

3. What tools may be used to apply base?

4. Olive and ruddy are elements of what?

5. Do all bases have the same amount of coverage?

6. What type of base gives the most amount of coverage ?

7. If a base is too pink, what color would you add?

8. When matching a base, should the color disappear?

9. Shade represents what in a base?

10. Undertone represents what in a base?

CHAPTER 4

CORRECTIVE MAKE-UP ————————————

The corrective process is an advanced technique using the corrective theory and methods utilizing shadows, highlights and color correctives (concealers) to negate the negative effects of shadows, highlights and colors that appear irregularly on the face.

The base application process is the first step in creating a beauty make-up, followed by the corrective techniques. With the addition of corrective techniques the make-up artist will be able to significantly improve the facial appearance.

After completing this chapter the artist will be able to correct, conceal and camouflage most negative aspects of the face.

SCULPTURAL LIGHT

The first step is to study the principles of light and shade (chiaroscuro) in theory, and observe them in the world around us. Then, apply these techniques in the application of make-up.

The key for all corrective make-up techniques lies in the understanding and application of light and shade. Just as an artist uses and manipulates light and shade to give the illusion of three-dimensional objects, in the same way the make-up artist must manipulate light and shade to correct certain negative shadows and highlights appearing on the face. When one looks at the face, what the eyes see is totally dependent on how the light is reflected from the surface of the face. Because each face is shaped differently, every face will reflect light in different patterns.

Artists who paint portraits have the ability to position the light anywhere they want. This does not mean that the artist paints a lamp in the picture, but that the artist places the highlights and shadows on the face according to the position of the light. If the artist does not highlight and shadow the painting according to the light source, the painting will not look very real. As make-up artists, we are

faced with a similar situation, but we do not have the ability to place the light anywhere we want. We must generally place the light source in front and above our model. The reason is, the performer is moving and acting within a three-dimensional world. If we did move the light source we would have shadows all over the face. When asked where to place a highlight or a shadow, the answer lies within another question: Where is the light? Once the artist understands where the light source is (generally in front of and above the actor), the artist will know where to place the highlight and shadow.

THE TWO-DIMENSIONAL WORLD

It is of utmost importance that the artist fully understand the difference between the three-dimensional world and the two-dimensional world of film and television.

Turn toward a mirror, and notice that the image of yourself is really flat and without shape. Notice that you see only the front half of yourself. You cannot see around yourself. You are really seeing yourself two-dimensionally, or only 180° of yourself. Next, hold a finger in front of your face closing one eye. Your finger moves from side to side as you switch eyes. This is happening because having two eyes gives us the ability to tell depth, allowing us to see the curvature of, and slightly around, objects. In essence, we have the ability to see more than half of an object. Height, width and depth are the three dimensions that we see.

A three-dimensional camera is actually two cameras bolted together at the same distance apart as human eyes. The right side records in one color and the left side records in another. When an object is placed in front of the cameras, the right camera is shooting it from the same perspective as our right eye would see it and the left camera is shooting the same object from the left eye's perspective.

In order to see the finished product three-dimensionally the viewer must wear special glasses that allow the information to process to the proper eyes, with the illusion then being completed in one's mind.

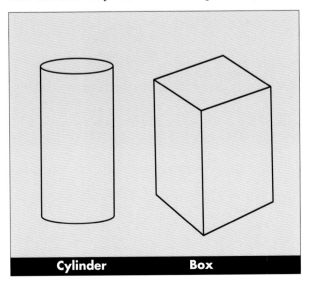

Cylinder   **Box**

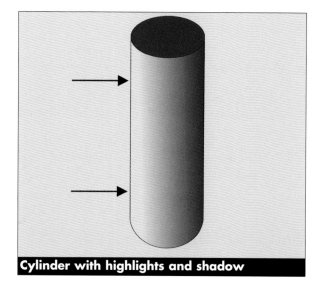

Cylinder with highlights and shadow

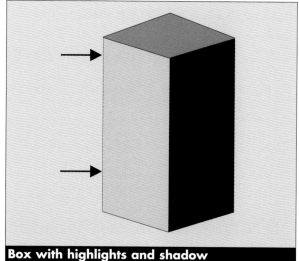

Box with highlights and shadow

A regular camera records everything through one lens and then is projected onto a flat screen. This is why film and television are only two-dimensional. What this means to the make-up artist is, we can fool the audience into believing they are seeing something that may only be painted on the face as opposed to really being there. The audience does not have the ability to see the depth but rather the illusion of depth created by the make-up artist.

FLAT AND CURVED SURFACES

Look at two objects, a box and a cylinder. The outline of the two objects may give a clue, but it is the way the shadows and highlights are reflected that make it possible to determine the true shape of the two objects.

If these two objects were observed in total darkness, then one would see nothing. Light provides the only means of seeing these objects. As these objects become illuminated by a light source, from the direction of the arrows, the light falls on the objects and is reflected back to the eyes. This effect makes it possible for the viewer to see them.

Observe how the light does not fall on these objects evenly. The surface areas that do not receive light are in darkness (shadow), and those areas where the light falls directly are fully visible. In the case of the cylinder, there is a gradual increase of shadow as the surface curves away from the light source. This is the same gradual transition as found in the gray scale. This effect makes it possible for the viewer to determine what direction the light is coming from and whether the surface is flat, curved or irregular. This information reveals the shape of an object.

Observe both the cylinder and box in the illustration. A portion of the objects are in shadow and highlight. However, the pattern of light and shadow are reflected differently on the cylinder and the box. The cylinder has a gradual shift from light to shadow. This indicates, to the viewer, that the cylinder has a curved surface. On the box there is a sudden shift from light to dark. This indicates, to the viewer, that the object has a flat surface with hard, sharp corners/edges.

The sharp division between highlight and shadow is known as a hard edge, and the gradual shift between highlight and shadow is known as a soft edge. These two shadow and highlight patterns apply directly to corrective make-up.

EXAMPLE
CYLINDER SHADOW PATTERN

Closely observe the shadow pattern of the cylinder. Arrow **W** indicates the lightest area on the cylinder. This is the area that receives the strongest consideration of light. Arrow **X** indicates the area which receives just a small amount of light. Arrow **Y** indicates the area that is slightly darker. Arrow **Z** is the darkest area and receives no light. As the surface curves away from the light source it gradually receives less light. Notice that the deepest shadow is on the opposite side of the light source.

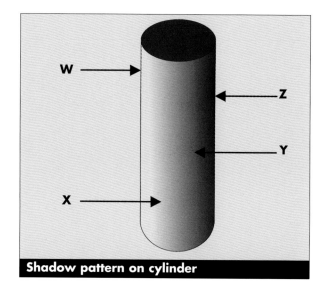

Shadow pattern on cylinder

EXAMPLE
NASOLABIAL FOLD

The nasolabial fold is usually the largest wrinkle pattern on the face. The nasolabial fold extends from outside the nostril area of the nose, down to the corners of the lips. A well-developed nasolabial fold, such as the one in the illustration, creates a fold or crease in the skin. This fold is created by a hard edge of shadow, arrow **A** next to a hard edge of highlight, arrow **B.** The outside of the fold fades out gradually, arrow **C.** This highlight and shadow pattern is the same as the highlight and shadow pattern on the cylinder. There is a gradual transition from the hard edge, at the crease, to a soft edge, on the outside of the wrinkle.

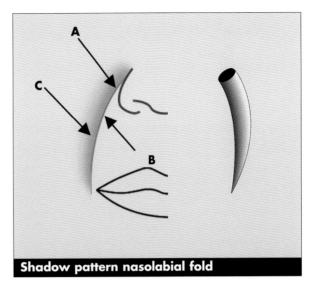

Shadow pattern nasolabial fold

EXAMPLE
SOFT EDGE TO SOFT EDGE SHADOW PATTERN

The **Soft Edge/Soft Edge** shadow pattern does not produce wrinkles, because there is no hard edge. Notice how the light does not fall evenly on the object. The surface areas that do not receive light are in shadow, and those areas the light falls on directly are fully visible. In the case of this object, there is a gradual increase of shadow as the surface curves away from the light. This is the gradual transition from light to shadow that can be found in the gray scale.

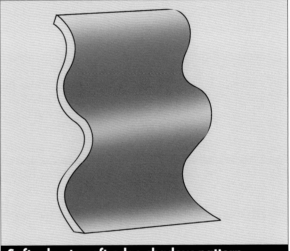

Soft edge to soft edge shadow pattern

EXAMPLE
SOFT EDGE TO SOFT EDGE -LABELED

The highlight begins at position **A,** then gradually darkens to position **B.** At position **C,** the shadow becomes its darkest. All the shadows and highlights have a gradual shift from highlights to shadows for a **Soft Edge/Soft Edge** effect.

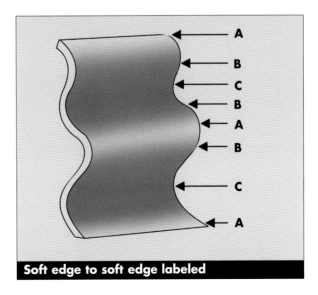

Soft edge to soft edge labeled

HIGHLIGHTS AND SHADOW

EXAMPLE

FACE WITH SHADOW-FRONT VIEW

Everyone's face and head is shaped and sized differently. Because of this fact, the following highlight and shadow patterns may vary from individual to individual.

This shadow pattern applies directly to corrective make-up. Notice the cheekbone. There is highlight on the top of the cheekbone and shadow below the cheekbone, and all the highlights and shadows are soft edges. The cheekbone resembles the cylinder, without the hard edges.

The forehead reflects highlight and shadow patterns of soft edges. This pattern produces an uneven effect on the forehead. Of course, the shadow pattern for the forehead will be different for everyone. By moving a finger across the forehead, one will feel high areas and low areas. The raised areas on the forehead tend to reflect more light than the lower areas, or depressions. Depressions tend to be in shadow because these depressed areas receive less light, so they reflect less light. This gives an uneven look to the forehead, as with other areas of the face. As one ages, these shadow and highlight areas become more pronounced.

Highlights and shadows can be created with a variety of products and application techniques.

CREAM APPLICATION

Once the base has been applied highlights and shadows may be added using cream products.

Highlights: Lighter shades of base in the same undertone series may be used in the highlight positions, or a product designed specifically for highlighting may be used. Generally these products

will have a tint of yellow or orange in them. Highlight colors can be blended into the base by mixing together on a palette. A small amount of the appropriate shade (lighter than the base) may be mixed with the base to achieve a base-tone relationship. These products may also be used on their own, in small amounts over the base, then blended into the base with a sponge. When the product is used is strictly dependent upon the effect to be achieved.

Shadows: Shadow colors work best when there is a small amount of gray in the shading color. Darker shades of base in the same undertone series may also be used in the shadow positions. Shadow colors should be blended into the base. A small amount of the appropriate shadow color may be mixed with the base to achieve a base-tone relationship.

Setting the base: After the application of cream products the base must be powdered to set the make-up. A colorless loose powder works well and will not change the overall color of the cream products already applied.

POWDER APPLICATION

Once the base has been applied the base must be completely set with loose powder, prior to the application of powdered highlights and shadows. Powder will slide over powder, providing a consistent surface for the application of powdered products.

Highlights: Some cosmetic companies make powdered highlights and shadow products, but when they are not available lighter shades of eye shadow or cheek color may be used as highlight. When using these products it is important to build the application in small increments. This will give the make-up artist complete control over the application. Keep in mind, it is much easier to add more product if needed than to have to remove excess unwanted product.

Shadows: Darker shades of eye shadow containing some gray, will work very well. When using powder products for shadowing, it is important to build the application in small increments.

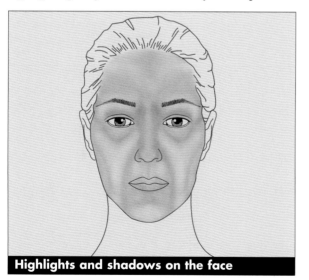

Highlights and shadows on the face

EXAMPLE
NEGATIVE HARD EDGE/SOFT EDGE

It is up to the make-up artist to balance out the uneven surface of the face. This is done by placing highlights and shadows to counteract negative highlights and shadows, such as pushing in an unwanted raised area and/or pulling out an unwanted depression.

When correcting a **negative shadow pattern**, it is necessary to use a highlight or a color lighter than the base color. A color lighter than the base will reflect more light than the darker base color since the shadow on the face reflects less light than the other areas of the face.

By applying highlighting color to the area in shadow, the highlight color will reflect more light, thereby reducing or eliminating the effect of the shadow in the highlighted area.

The highlight color should have a base-tone relationship. This base-tone relationship means that the base and the highlight have the same, or very close to the same, undertone. For example: If the artist applies a base with an olive undertone, then the highlight should have the same olive undertone. If the artist uses a highlighting color that has a ruddy undertone, then the highlighting color and the base will not blend together.

Refer to the base worksheets in the base chapter to determine what may be used as highlight for a particular base.

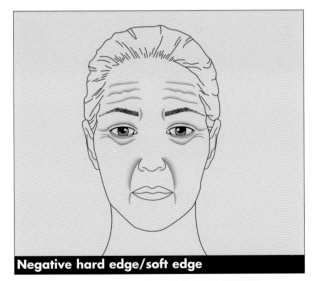

Negative hard edge/soft edge

THE NASOLABIAL FOLD CORRECTION

The nasolabial fold consists of a hard edge and a soft edge.

The highlight should be placed on the shadow. A hard edge of highlight should be placed on the hard edge of shadow, arrow **A**. As the shadow begins to fade, so should the highlight, arrow **B**, in direct proportion to the fade of the shadow.

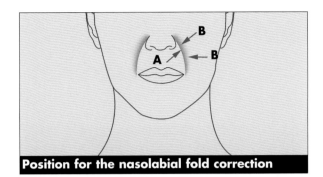

Position for the nasolabial fold correction

Be careful that the hard edge of highlight does not extend past the hard edge of shadow. If this happens, the corrective effect of the highlight will be canceled out.

Application:

The highlight color may be applied using a **small eye shadow brush or concealer brush.** To load the brush, place a small amount of product on the palette. Stroke the brush across the product, evenly distributing product to both sides of the brush. Place the brush at the top hard edge of the nasolabial fold, and drag the brush down along the hard edge to the end of the shadow. With the brush, gently blend the highlight on the shadow fading the highlight as the shadow fades. Be sure to keep the hard edge of highlight hard.

THE EYE POUCH CORRECTION

The eye pouch shadow position is corrected in the same way as the nasolabial fold. A hard edge of highlight arrow **A**, should be placed on the hard edge of shadow, and blended off as the shadow blends off, arrow **B**.

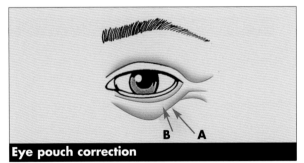

Eye pouch correction

UPPER LID CORRECTION

On the upper outside corner of the eyelid there is a shadow pattern that causes the drooping eye effect. This drooping effect becomes more dramatic as a hard edge develops.

The corrective pattern begins by placing a hard edge of highlight on the hard edge of shadow, arrow **A**, and blending off as the shadow fades, arrow **B**.

All negative shadow patterns with a hard edge may be corrected in this way.

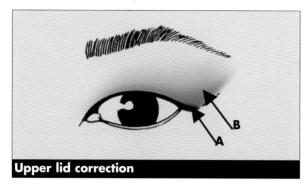
Upper lid correction

EYE LEDGE CORRECTION

This shadow position occurs when the area just under the eye is recessed or slightly behind the lower orbital rim. This position causes a hard edge of shadow at the point where the orbital rim and the tissue just below the eye meet. At this point the shadow begins to fade down, away from the eye.

The correction follows the same pattern as with all hard edge/soft edge shadow patterns. Place a hard edge of highlight, arrow **A**, on the hard edge of shadow, and blend off the highlight as the shadow softens, arrow **B**.

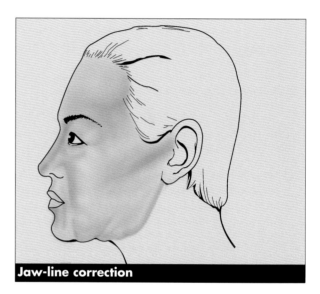
Jaw-line correction

Eye ledge correction

JAW LINE CORRECTION

Using shadow in combination with highlight will help in defining the jaw-line, the nose, and the cheekbone.

Application:

The shadow areas can be corrected with the use of highlight, arrow **A**. However, there will be occasions when the use of shadow may be necessary, arrow **B**. Because of the drooping area, the jaw-line may catch highlight just below the jaw-line.

A soft edge of shadow may be applied to the areas in order to straighten the jaw-line. Make sure that there are no hard edges of shadow. Remember to blend, blend, blend!

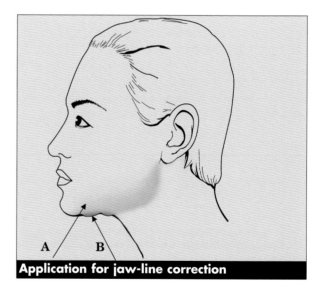
Application for jaw-line correction

CHEEKBONE CORRECTIONS

You can correct or accentuate the cheekbone with the use of highlight and shadow.

As shown in the cheekbone cylinder illustration the cheekbone shadow and highlight pattern is similar to the cylinder. With the proper placement of highlight and shadow, the illusion of a defined cheekbone may be created.

Application:

First, locate the lower area of the cheekbone. This may be done by using a finger. Press your finger along the bottom of the cheekbone. Generally, commencing at the center of the ear will give you a good position to start from. There will be a noticeable depression or turn created by the bottom of the cheekbone, arrow **A**. This is where the shadow will be placed.

The cheekbone will extend from the ear to the outside corner of the eye. Now, with your finger, find the top edge of the cheekbone, arrow B. This is where the highlight will be placed. Follow the edge from the hair line to approximately the outside corner of the eye. If you are having difficulty locating the cheekbone (as in someone with a full facial shape) you may start at the front where the cheekbone curves and follow it back toward the ear.

The position, width and length of the cheekbone will vary from person to person.

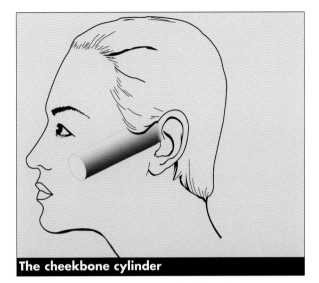

The cheekbone cylinder

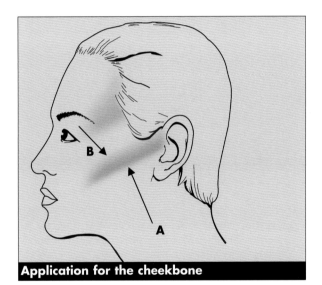

Application for the cheekbone

NOSE CORRECTIONS

Noses come in all shapes and sizes: big, small, long, short, wide bridge, narrow bridge, sharp bridge, soft bridge, etc. Analyzing the nose from both a profile and front view, the make-up artist can make subtle, and sometimes dramatic, changes in the appearance of the nose. There are also things that cannot be changed, such as the profile view of the nose. Most visible changes will be seen from the front view.

Changing the nose shape is done for a couple of reasons. First, to balance out the overall shape of the nose, which in doing so can give balance to the entire face. Another reason to highlight and shadow a nose may be simply to give dimension to the nose for a particular lighting condition. Remember, film and television are two-dimensional.

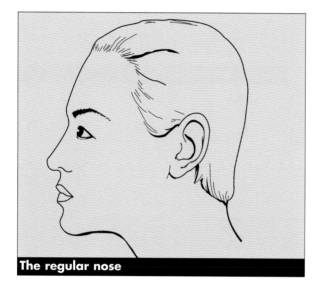

The regular nose

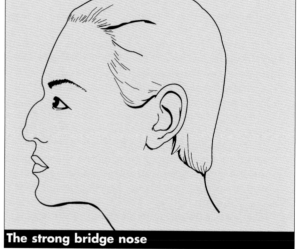

The strong bridge nose

Regular Nose: From the profile view the nose is balanced to the face. Use this illustration to compare the strong bridge nose and the flat nose.

Strong Bridge: No amount of shadow or concealer can disguise the fact that there is a bump on the nose.

Flat Nose: No amount of highlight will make the nose appear to have a stronger bridge from the profile.

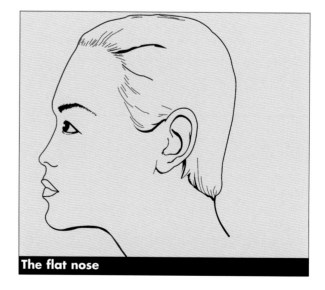

The flat nose

These illustrations show the effective use of high-light and shadow to correct and accentuate the nose.

PROBLEM:
The Flat Nose
In this illustration of the flat nose there is no definition to the orbital area or the nose bridge.

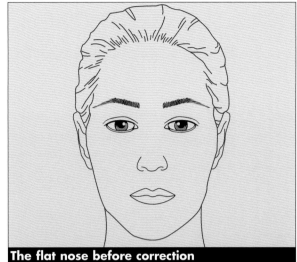
The flat nose before correction

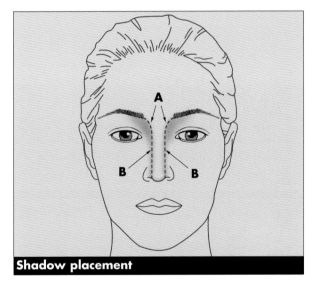
Shadow placement

RESULT:
The illusion of a stronger bridge and deeper orbital rim areas give balance and definition to the nose as well as to the face.

CORRECTION:
• Using a Small Eye Shadow Brush apply the shadow, beginning at the eyebrow and curving around the inside of the orbital rim, arrow **A**. Follow in a straight line down the side of the nose, arrow **B**. Repeat process on opposite side of the nose.

• At the inner corner of the eye, just under the eyebrow, notice that the shadow deepens. This gives the effect of a stronger bridge area, creating depth to the orbital rim. The top and bottom edges of the shadow are soft.

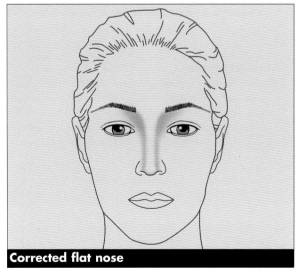
Corrected flat nose

PROBLEM:
The Triangular Nose
The triangular nose is narrow at the bridge area, between the eyes, and wider at the tip. This results in an out-of-balance appearance.

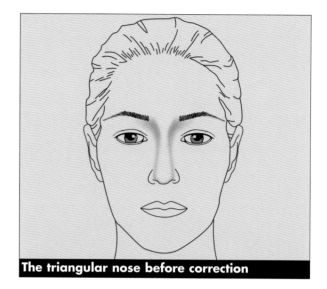

The triangular nose before correction

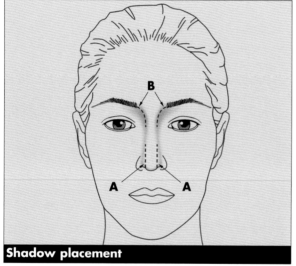

Shadow placement

RESULT:
The triangular nose is now widened at the bridge area between the eyes, and narrowed at the tip, bringing the nose into balance.

CORRECTION:
The make-up artist should narrow the tip of the nose, and widen the bridge of the nose between the eyes. This is done by applying shadow to the tip of the nose on either side (see arrow **A**) and, highlighting the nose in the two shadow positions (arrow **B**)

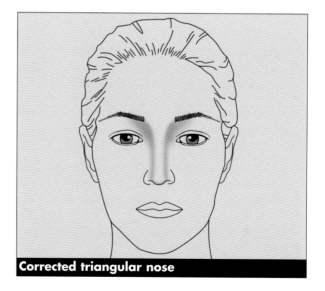

Corrected triangular nose

PROBLEM:
The Crooked Nose

The crooked nose is a nose that has a bend or turn. (See crooked nose illustration.) In this illustration the nose bends from the viewer's left to right. The shadow pushes in on the right side, and the highlight pulls out on the left.

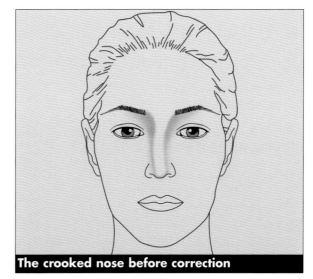
The crooked nose before correction

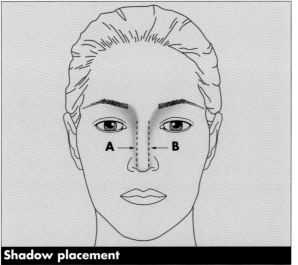
Shadow placement

RESULT:

The crooked nose is now straightened, bringing the nose into balance.

CORRECTION:

To correct this, the make-up artist must apply shadow along the bend where the highlight pulls out. See arrow **A**. Then apply highlight where the shadow pushes in. See arrow **B**.

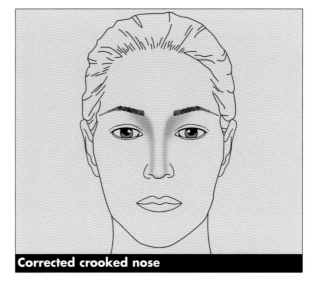
Corrected crooked nose

PROBLEM:
The Bulbous Nose

The bulbous nose has a rounded or ball-like tip. This creates an unbalanced nose bringing undue attention to the spherical grandeur of the nose.

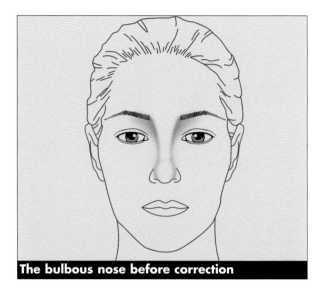
The bulbous nose before correction

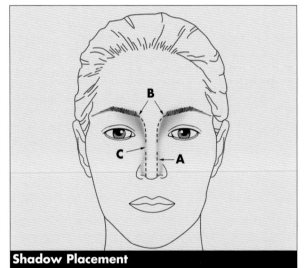
Shadow Placement

RESULT:

The bulbous nose is now narrowed at the bridge area between the eyes, and narrowed at the tip, bringing the nose into balance.

CORRECTION:

The tip of the nose should be shaded on either side, and blended to a soft edge. See arrow **A**. This should correct most bulbous noses. Sometimes the bridge will need correction. To achieve this, arrow **B** should be shaded to bring the bridge between the eyes in balance. Between the tip and the upper bridge the nose pinches in slightly. Highlight should be placed at arrow **C**. The highlight is applied along the bridge line and blended towards the top of the nose. The bottom edge of highlight should be softened slightly.

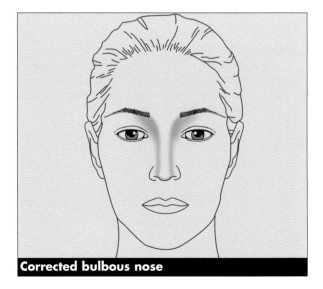
Corrected bulbous nose

PROBLEM:

Irregular Nose Shadow:

This shadow pattern appears when there is a depression on the nose. (See the irregular nose shadow illustration.) There may be one or more depressions in various positions on the nose.

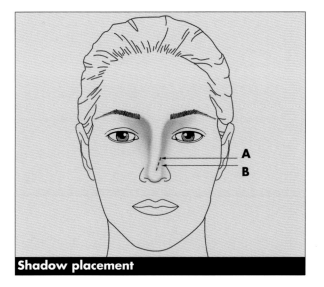

Shadow placement

CORRECTION:

These shadows may be reduced or eliminated by applying highlight to the darkest area of the shadow, arrow **A**, and blending to the soft edges, arrow **B**.

The irregular nose shadow before correction

RESULT:

The depression of the irregular nose is now pulled forward, bringing the nose into balance.

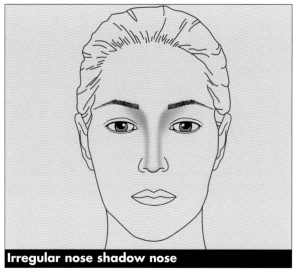

Irregular nose shadow nose

PROBLEM:
Shadowed Nose Bridge

Observe the shadow on the nose bridge, between the eyes. See the shadowed nose bridge illustration. This is a common problem, caused by a depression on the nose.

This depression catches shadows and causes the brow ridge to appear too strong because of the contrast between the highlight and the brow ridge, arrow **B**, and the deep shadow, arrow **A**.

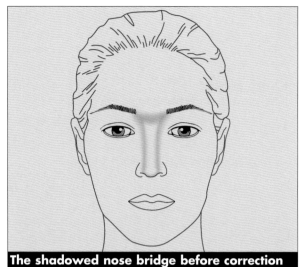

The shadowed nose bridge before correction

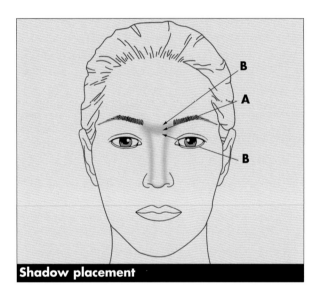

Shadow placement

RESULT:

The effects of this shadow are eliminated or reduced by applying highlight on the shadow.

CORRECTION:

Blend off the highlight to soften edges above and below, arrow **B**, as the shadow fades out. The highlight should remain strongest at the deepest area of shadow, arrow **A**.

Be very careful when blending the highlight at the brow ridge, arrow **B**. If the highlight is placed too high, the correction effect will be lost and the brow ridge will remain heavy in appearance.

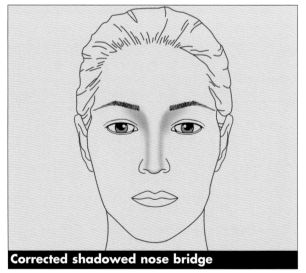

Corrected shadowed nose bridge

PROBLEM:

Narrow Nose

The narrow nose is the most challenging to correct. The bridge of the narrow nose is thin. From the frontal view, the sides of the nose are usually not fully visible. This limits the make-up artist's options for corrective placement, because the surface area needed to widen the nose is limited or not available.

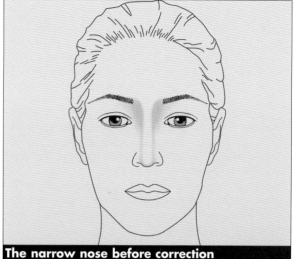

The narrow nose before correction

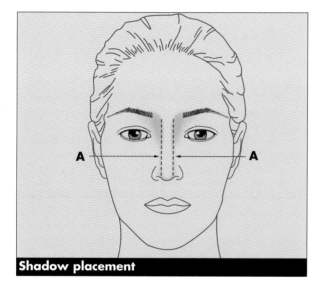

Shadow placement

CORRECTION:

The narrow nose may be corrected by applying a narrow soft-edge highlight along the sides of the nose, arrow **A**. Do not blend the highlight over or on top of the nose bridge. The position of the highlight must remain tight, and blended to the natural highlights of the bridge area.

RESULT:

The narrow nose is now widened, bringing the nose into balance.

NOTE:

Each person's face is unique, and, therefore, each face will require different corrective measures. Analyze the face to find the areas in need of balance. Analyze the face from both a profile and front view.

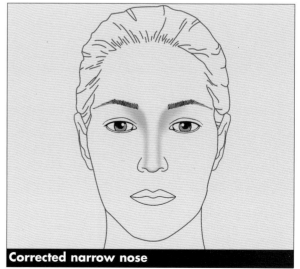

Corrected narrow nose

CONCEALERS, CAMOUFLAGE, COUNTER BALANCE AND COLOR THEORY

Quite often there are several names for the same thing. This is the case with corrective make-up. At one point or another you will hear all of the different terminologies that apply. **Concealers** are used to **camouflage** or **conceal** an area that is unwanted. In doing this the artist has in effect **counter-balanced** the color of the unwanted area. With that in mind, for the remainder of this section the product will be referred to as a concealer.

It is important to have an understanding of basic color theory to successfully conceal problematic areas of discoloration. For this we will be referring to the artist's color wheel.

There are three **primary** colors: blue, yellow and red. These are stand-alone colors or colors that have not come from mixing other colors together. Next on the color wheel are the three **secondary** colors: orange, violet and green. These colors come from mixing two of the primary colors together.

- Mixing primary colors red and yellow make a secondary color-**orange**

- Mixing primary colors red and blue make a secondary color-**violet**

- Mixing primary colors yellow and blue make a secondary color-**green**

Next are the six **tertiary** or **intermediate** colors. Red-orange, yellow-orange, yellow-green, blue-green, blue-violet and red-violet. These colors come from mixing a **primary** color with a **secondary** color.

How this information relates to concealers: Certain colors will neutralize or cancel out other colors.

Examples of this would be:
- **Orange** cancels **blue**, therefore concealing or camouflaging blue.

- **Green** cancels **red**, therefore concealing or camouflaging red.

- **Yellow** cancels **violet**, therefore concealing or camouflaging violet.

The primary purpose of a concealer is to correct negative color problems. Where might the artist find these negative color problems on the face?

- Blemishes are usually a shade of red. A concealer with green in it will work to cancel out red.

- Circles under the eyes may be a shade of blue or a shade of violet. Or perhaps a blue-violet. A concealer with orange in it will work to cancel out blue.

A concealer with yellow in it will work to cancel out violet.

- Or a combination of orange and yellow will cancel out blue-violet.

Another factor to consider when using concealers, is the shade of the skin. The concealer should be a close match to the shade of the skin, not the shade of the discoloration. When correcting dark blue or violet colors under the eye, match the surrounding skin color not the darkness of the discoloration. If the darkness of the discoloration is matched, then there will be a dark circle of concealer under the eye, instead of the dark blue or violet.

The same thing will happen when correcting blemishes or acne discoloration. Match the shade of the skin, not the discoloration. If the shade of the blemish is matched there will be dark areas of concealers. One correction problem will be exchanged for another. The two factors needed to successfully conceal are the color of the problem area and the shade of the skin tone.

Concealer may also be used, depending on shade and color, as a Highlight and/or Shadow. Concealers usually have a higher concentration of pigment and/or waxes to increase coverage.

Concealers may be applied before or after the base depending on the degree or depth of the problem area to be corrected. Most often the base will be applied first and then any concealers that are needed applied on top of the base. The base often will take care of a majority of the unevenness or discoloration in the skin tone. As with most make-up applications, use a concealer only when necessary, using a small amount of product and building as necessary.

Application:
After the base application, analyze the face for any negative color problems. Look under the eyes, and the inside corners of the eyes, then check for any blemishes on the face or neck. Referring to the Color Theory section, choose a concealer that will counter-balance the color problem and match the skin tone. For a general application, use a small eye shadow brush, small concealer brush or sponge to apply. The brush application is the most accurate. A light tapping motion works well and will not lift any base that has previously been applied. Remember to use less, adding more if necessary. Using the sponge that was used to apply the base, lightly roll over the area where the concealer is, in order to blend the concealer into the base; do this gently, being careful not to lift the product onto the sponge.

If the correction is minor, load concealer on the brush and lightly paint the concealer over the area to be corrected.

If the correction requires a heavier application use a brush but, in this case, use the flat side of the brush with a patting motion over the area to be corrected. This patting application will build up more product. Use only as much as necessary, especially on the eye area. If the under-eye area requires a heavier application, monitor this because of possible creasing. If this occurs, pat with the brush until the creases are eliminated, then powder.

CHAPTER STUDY QUESTIONS

1. Chiaroscuro is the study of?

2. Does corrective make-up allow the artist to correct all problematic areas?

3. What color will orange conceal?

4. A blemish is what color?

5. In choosing a concealer color what must be factors?

6. All nose corrections require highlight and shadow?

7. A wrinkle has both a hard and soft edge?

8. When using a concealer it is best to use a lot?

9. The soft edge to soft edge shadow pattern has hard edges?

10. Does every make-up require concealer?

CHAPTER 5

EYEBROWS

For a flattering, natural and balanced eyebrow the make-up artist needs to be able to recognize different styles of eyebrows and determine which brow shapes work best for each individual. The make-up artist will be able to shape the eyebrow, while maintaining a natural appearance to the eyebrows and the face. The make-up artist will observe how changing the shape of the eyebrows can affect a person's expression – open or close down the eye, lift up or pull down the face.

PHYSICAL FEATURES OF THE EYEBROW

It has been said that the eyes are the window to the soul. Much effort is spent choosing colors, shadow placement, liner position, mascara and brushes, just as an artist labors over his painting.

The artist would not think of displaying his work of art without carefully choosing the proper frame to enhance and bring focus to his painting. Without a frame, no importance would be given to the painting; a bad frame would detract from its beauty.

The same is true of the eyes. Without the eyebrows there is no focus to them; and a badly placed or shaped eyebrow will detract from the eye as well as the make-up.

The Eyebrow consists of a group of hairs that grow above the eye on the frontal bone. The eyebrow provides the upper frame of the eye, while the upper cheekbone, also known as the zygomatic arch, provides the lower frame. Together, this makes the eye a focal point of the face.

In analyzing the face you will notice that humans are not symmetrical. Eyebrows are rarely exactly the same on any one individual. They can vary from slight to extreme. It is the make-up artist's job to make them as similar as possible, not exact.

The parts of the eyebrow consist of the Inner Brow, the Arch (Peak and Base) and the Outer Brow.

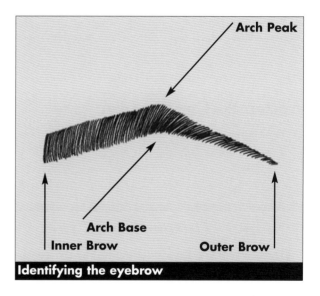

Arch Peak
Arch Base
Inner Brow
Outer Brow

Identifying the eyebrow

PLACEMENT OF THE CLASSIC EYEBROW

The Classic Eyebrow is very reminiscent of an eyebrow shape of the 1950's. Although the eyebrows of the 50's were perhaps a bit sharper on the edges, they were, and remain today, a "classic" shape.

The make-up artist will need to assess each person to determine which of the many possible shapes will be the most flattering to that individual. Women and men need occasional eyebrow grooming to control and maintain a well balanced eyebrow.

Placement of the eyebrow is achieved by adding to or subtracting from the eyebrow. This process is achieved by tweezing, or removing, unwanted hair, and filling in areas where eyebrows are needed.

Certain eyebrow placements will make the model appear angry, sad, surprised and so on. Some placements will make the eyes appear closer together, while others will make the eyes appear farther apart.

At first glance, the options for the eyebrows appear to be infinite. Which options should be used?

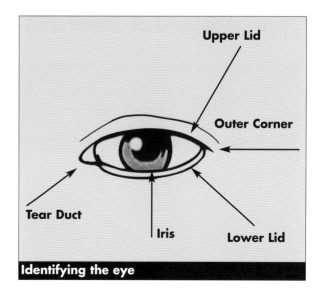

Upper Lid
Outer Corner
Tear Duct
Iris
Lower Lid

Identifying the eye

There is an eyebrow position that solves these problems: the benchmark position, or standard measurement, should be the Classic Eyebrow.

The Classic Eyebrow is the touchstone. It will be the gage by which we discuss eyebrow placement, problems, and solutions. From this basic position all other eyebrow shapes can be achieved by slightly altering thickness or thinness, angle or roundness of the arch and where the eyebrow begins and ends.

There are seven basic steps by which a standard of measurement is used for placing the Classic Eyebrow. This is a guideline. It does not mean that every person should or will have this eyebrow shape. Some will have a version of the Classic Eyebrow, such as the Natural or the Thin Eyebrow. A person's facial structure or the character to be created are determining factors in choosing an eyebrow shape. By understanding these steps, the mysteries of the eyebrow may be understood.

There are several parts of the eye itself that are involved in determining the positioning of the Classic Eyebrow. They are the Tear Duct, Iris, Lower Lid, Upper Lid and the Outside Corner.

Step 1– Inner Brow Line

The inside placement (or beginning) of the eyebrow is determined by the **inner brow line**, which extends from the tear duct upward.

Step 2– Center Line

The center and **arch (peak and base)** position is determined by the **center line**, which extends from the outside edge of the iris upward.

Step 3– Outer Brow Line

The **outer brow line** is determined by the distance from the **inner brow line** to the **center line**, which is approximately an equal distance from the **arch (peak and base)** to the **outer brow line.**

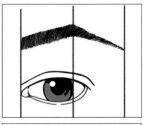

Step 4– Upper & Lower Lid Lines

The horizontal position of the eyebrow is determined by the width of the eye opening, between the **upper lid** and the **lower lid**.

Step 5– Brow Line

The Classic Eyebrow begins one full **"open eye"** above the **upper lash** of the eye. This is the **brow line**.

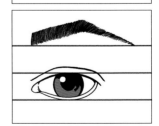

Step 6– Arch Peak

The **arch peak** is approximately another full **"open eye"** from the base of the brow.

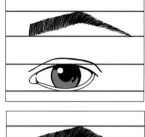

Step 7– Arch Base Line

The **arch base** is approximately **half** the horizontal distance of the **"open eye."** The same distance is also the height of the eyebrow, from the inner brow line to the center.

Completed Classic Eyebrow

The seven steps complete the graph for the Classic Eyebrow Position. It is important to note the direction of the hair growth within the sections of the graph.

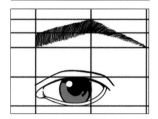

GROWTH PATTERN OF THE CLASSIC EYEBROW

The hairs of the eyebrow grow in a very definite growth pattern, starting at inner brow. The hairs grow from the bottom of the eyebrow up. Hair growth at the inner brow is slightly angled, and as it proceeds toward the arch or center of the brow, the hair angles slightly more than the one before it. At the arch, the growth takes on a more dramatic angle, with the hairs progressively getting flatter as the brow goes to the outer brow.

The thickest portion of hair is at the inner brow, with the hairs narrowing as they go towards the arch and tapering more from the arch to the outer brow. This taper will become a very fine point.

Generally, there is equal distance between the individual hairs of the eyebrows. In drawing the eyebrow it is best to follow the growth pattern of the eyebrow; start at the inner brow, continue up to the arch, then down to the outer brow. This will give the make-up artist a consistent pattern to follow and may be used on anyone no matter what shape eyebrow is desired.

SHAPING THE EYEBROW

Because the face is not symmetrical, one eyebrow generally will not be the same as the other. The idea in shaping eyebrows is not necessarily to make them exactly the same, but to make them look as close in shape and equal in weight as possible.

There should be one eye width between the eyebrows (above the nose) for equal spacing. If there is less width, the eyes may appear closed in; if there is more width, the eyes may appear too far apart, and both of them will be out of balance.

Facing a mirror, analyzing the eyebrows by sitting in as natural a light as possible. Be objective, analyze both eyebrows for overall positioning and balance.

Answer the following questions:

- Do the eyebrows appear heavy or over-powering?
- Are the eyebrows hardly noticeable, or too light?
- Is there a natural arch to the eyebrow or are the eyebrows flat?
- Are the eyebrows too round, without much of an arch?
- Is there a balanced space between the eyebrows above the nose?
- Are there holes or gaps in the eyebrow?
- Are there extra long hairs that extend up or down in the eyebrows?
- Are both eyebrows at the same elevation above the eyes?

These issues are easily resolved by shaping the eyebrow.

Shaping the eyebrow involves several elements, which can be used in combination or separately. This is determined by the condition or shape of the existing eyebrow together with the desired shape.

These elements include: brushing, trimming, and tweezing.

Brushing is used to maneuver the hair in the direction of the hair growth. This will show the make-up artist where hairs need to be tweezed or trimmed.

Tweezing is used to remove individual hairs that are interfering with the desired shape.

Trimming is used to control hair length and thickness. Hairs that extend past the desired shape will need to be trimmed.

BRUSHING

Brushing the eyebrow allows the artist to see what, if any, hairs might need to be removed or trimmed to achieve a flattering and open appearance to the eye. Using a brow brush, brush the hairs of the eyebrow in an upward motion, starting at the inner brow line. Work toward the arch in short concise strokes changing the angle of the brush once the arch peak has been reached. From the arch peak, work toward the outer brow line, brushing up and out to the outer brow line. Using the Classic Eyebrow shape as a guide, determine which hairs need to be removed or trimmed to achieve this shape. Next, brush the hairs down, trimming those that extend below the Classic Eyebrow shape.

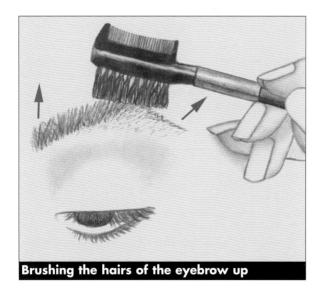

Brushing the hairs of the eyebrow up

TRIMMING

After brushing the eyebrows, determine whether there are any wild or extremely long hairs that need to be trimmed. The shears should be kept sharp to lower the risk of possibly pulling out hairs. Referring again to the Classic Eyebrow shape, trim the eyebrow across the top of the eyebrow only if necessary.

Trimming the eyebrows can be done using a small pair of shears. Hold the open shears at a slight angle, with the outside edge of the back blade against the forehead. The tip of the shears should be pointing up. Begin trimming at the outer brow line on top of the eyebrow. Trim up to the arch peak. Change shear position. The tip of the shears should be pointing down. Then, from the arch peak work down to the top of the eyebrow at the inner brow line.

Next, brush the hairs down. Begin at the outer brow line under the eyebrow. Trim away any excess length up to the arch base. Change the angle of the shears to point down and trim from the arch base to the inner brow line. Check the work, and repeat with the other eyebrow.

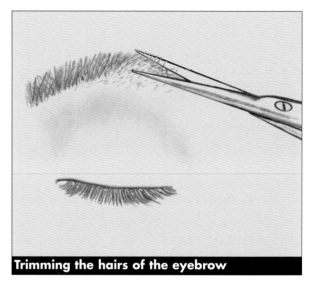

Trimming the hairs of the eyebrow

Trimming unruly hairs, combined with tweezing, can give the eyes a lift comparable to the Classic Eyebrow, creating a more defined arch peak. To determine what might need to be done, look at the overall shape.

Not all eyebrows will require trimming, but most will need some amount of tweezing.

The following illustrations demonstrate the four steps for trimming eyebrows.

Step 1

This brow shows hairs that are longer than desired, or outside the shape of the Classic Eyebrow.

Step 2

Shows where the guidelines are for the Classic Eyebrow

Step 3

Using an eyebrow brush, brush the hairs up towards the temple. Following the guideline for the Classic Eyebrow, trim only a few hairs at at time.

Step 4

Next, brush the hairs down and trim any excess hair length. Once this step has been completed, the make-up artist is now ready to tweeze any stray hairs.

TWEEZING

Tweezing is a method for removing hairs, using a tool called tweezers. Tweezers should be sturdy and have a defined, sharp, angled edge, allowing for a firm grip. Tweezing allows the make-up artist complete control, removing a single hair at a time. It is advisable not to remove the hair in clumps or clusters, as this can become uncomfortable for the model. It is recommended you tweeze between the eyebrows in order to create a clean and well manicured effect. When the eyebrow has a clean defined look the rest of the eye treatment (shadow and liner) will also be well defined.

Tweezing the eyebrow is done once trimming is complete. On a tissue or cotton pad, pour a small amount of 99% alcohol and gently wipe the area to be tweezed. This will cleanse the area, as well as slightly desensitize it. Be careful not to soak the tissue/cotton pad, or allow it to drip in or near the model's eyes.

Starting at the inner brow line, lift the skin taut by pulling up just above the brow. This will also aid in desensitizing the area, and will help lift the hairs away from the skin, making it easier to grip the hairs for removal.

Using the guidelines established by the Classic Eyebrow Chart, tweeze the area between the eyebrows by placing one side of the tweezers under the hair to be removed and squeezing the tweezers closed. Using quick small jerks, pull in the direction of the hair growth. As you tweeze, wipe the hairs from the tweezers on a clean tissue.

Next, move to the area underneath the eyebrow at the inner brow line and work toward the arch. Occasionally, wipe the area with the 99% alcohol while tweezing. If necessary, re-brush the eyebrow to maintain shape, continuing to pull the skin taut on the areas that are being worked on.

Next, move on to the arch base, tweezing to create a defined, uplifting arch. Once this has been accomplished, continue underneath the Eyebrow to the outer brow line.

Occasionally it is necessary to tweeze stray hairs on top of the eyebrow. Tweezing is a large part of shaping the eyebrow; this includes above and below the eyebrow.

Once finished, assess the shape and make any adjustments necessary. It is normal for the area that has been tweezed to become slightly reddened, but using the 99% alcohol will help minimize this. Witch Hazel may also be used in place of the 99% alcohol.

Check for balance and shape of the eyebrow, then repeat the process with the other eyebrow.

Ideally there should be one eye width between the brows. If there is less width, the eyes may appear closed in; if there is more width, the eyes may appear too far apart, and therefore out of balance.

A method that may help to see where to tweeze involves using a white pencil first, to color the hairs to be removed.

Tweezing the eyebrow

SHADING AND FILLING IN THE EYEBROW

After shaping the eyebrows, it may be necessary to add color (shading) by filling in the eyebrow. There are two different types of media that may be used for shading or filling in: an eyebrow pencil or a powder eye-shadow product.

As is the case with all make-up applications, filling in the eyebrow is done only when necessary. This can range from using a small amount of eye shadow/pencil on one eyebrow, to completely creating both eyebrows, using a combination of methods, where perhaps no eyebrows exist.

The amount and type of product chosen is dependent on the look to be achieved and color choices. Ideally, color choices should be made based upon the natural color of the eyebrow. When one color is not a match, colors can be mixed to create the appropriate shade.

Some eyebrows may be so naturally light in color that it is difficult to see their definition without the aid of filling in. This may be the case with blonde eyebrows. When working with eyebrows of this nature it is important to fill them in even if the shape is exactly what the artist is looking for, the reason being, that light eyebrows do not read well on camera. This is not to say that light eyebrows need to be made dark, just darkened enough to be seen in the mirror. The mirror will help to give the artist an idea of how the camera will see this image. Eyebrows that are naturally dark in color may not need any filling in, unless there are gaps in the hairs or the existing shape is not desired. If there are gaps in the hairs of the eyebrow this generally means that there will be skin showing through. The camera will see that skin. When the hair is dark, the skin will stand out and be quite noticeable.

Shading in the eyebrow enhances and, in some cases, produces the shape of the eyebrow. Filling in the eyebrow can add dimension, giving it a finished yet natural appearance.

Pencils can have a hard edge, creating the illusion of hair where there is none. Powders, when used dry, will have a much softer look. When used wet, powders can have a harder sharp edge, but are less defined than a pencil. The choice is strictly dependent upon the look and/or shape the make-up artist is trying to achieve.

EYEBROW PENCILS

Choose a shade that matches the natural color of the eyebrow or, if the hairs are very light, choose a shade that is slightly darker; one or more shades can be used to create dimension and realism.

Before using an eyebrow pencil it is important to sharpen it, using a pencil sharpener to produce a fine point. At this time it is also recommended the pencil be sprayed with 99% alcohol in order to keep it sanitary. With the tip of the pencil at a 45 degree angle, place the pencil next to the skin, starting at the bottom of the inner brow and working upward, drawing in small strokes to represent hair.

Filling in the eyebrow with pencil

For a realistic look, apply more pressure at the bottom of the stroke where the root would be. Ease off on the pressure as you flick your stroke up, in a slight, natural curve. If needed, the entire eyebrow can be drawn like this, following up to the arch peak with a graceful curve, and tapering to a fine point where the eyebrow should end. If the eyebrow is sparse, use this same technique to fill in where needed.

When using an eyebrow pencil, it is most important to keep the pencil sharp. This may need to done more than once during the filling-in procedure. A good rule of thumb is to do this as often as is needed.

POWDER EYE SHADOW

Another method that may be used to give shape to the eyebrows is a wet or dry application of eye shadow. For a softer look, use a dry application of powder eye shadow. For a defined look, use a wet application. Either method may be applied with an angle or wedge brush.

Dry Application

When using this method, load the brush by tapping the edge of the brush into the powder eye shadow. Do this gently, adding only a small amount at a time. It is much easier to add more product, if needed, than to have too much on the brush, requiring its removal.

Wet Application

Using the same application method as above, powder eye shadow may be used wet. This gives a sleek, more defined look. Once again using less product gives more control to the artist, as more product can be added as needed. Slightly dampen the brush with water and work the powder eye shadow into the brush, using a forward and then backward motion to load the brush evenly. This may need to be done several times throughout the application to keep the product moist on the brush.

Directions:

Once the brush is loaded, start at the inner brow line, laying the brush against the eyebrow with the wide edge of the brush directed down on an angle towards the nose. Keep an even amount of pressure on the brush while drawing in an upward direction. Work towards the arch. Once the arch has been reached, turn the brush so that the wide edge of the brush is up, with the small edge down. Work from the arch peak to the outer brow line, drawing to a tapered, fine point. Darkening some specific areas of the brow with a slightly darker shadow color will simulate real hairs.

Filling in the eyebrow with powder eye shadow

COLOR CHOICE

Choosing the proper color to fill in or enhance the eyebrows may depend on several variables. First, ask yourself what is the desired look you wish to achieve. Will this be a natural look? Are you creating a character for a role? What is the message in the look?

Choosing more than one color of product can add a more realistic look to the eyebrow, especially when the eyebrow and hair color are different.

The following are examples of color choices for a natural look. To be considered are the natural color of the model's eyebrows and the hair color.

EXAMPLE:
Eyebrows that are naturally light or blonde.

Color Choice: The eyebrows almost disappear, leaving the eye somewhat un-framed. Fill in with either a taupe or light warm brown shade. The eyebrows can now frame the eye, looking natural and soft. A shade too dark could overpower the eye. If in doubt, begin with a light shade and build by adding a slightly darker shade if necessary.

EXAMPLE:
Eyebrows that have good color, but have a few sparse areas.

Color Choice: Match the natural color of the brow, filling in only where needed to match the existing eyebrow.

EXAMPLE:
Red or auburn-colored hair.

Color Choice: If the hair color is a light reddish blonde, follow the same theory for blonde hair, adding a touch of an auburn shade as the additional shade. When the hair color is a medium red/auburn, add a medium brown with a sienna shade. For dark red/auburn hair, a warm medium cinnamon color can be quite effective.

EXAMPLE:
Dark brown eyebrows.

Color Choice: Attention must be given to avoid a harsh look. Choosing a dark brown instead of a black will help prevent this hard appearance. A dark brown combined with a medium brown will add an element of softness.

EXAMPLE:
Naturally black eyebrows.

Color Choice: Fill in only where it is necessary to create a well defined shape. Black combined with a dark brown can work well to avoid overpowering the eye.

EXAMPLE:
Excessively light skin tone.

Color Choice: Using a black shade to fill in eyebrows may appear harsh. Even if hair is very dark, use a dark to medium brown to soften the face.

VARIATIONS OF THE CLASSIC EYEBROW

Eyebrow shapes are customized to fit each individual's face. As previously mentioned, there are several styles of eyebrows. There are two styles with slight variations of the Classic Eyebrow. Each one is unique while adhering to the guidelines of the Classic Eyebrow.

Though the Classic Eyebrow works well with most individuals' face shape/size, occasionally a person can benefit from a variation of the Classic Eyebrow. If a person is petite with a delicate face, the **Thin Eyebrow** might be the better choice to maintain balance. If an individual has a sporty/athletic build, the **Natural Eyebrow** might be the better choice.

The Natural Eyebrow is characterized by a less defined yet somewhat clean edge. It is thicker, fuller, yet somewhat contained, with a soft arch.

The Thin Eyebrow is quite a bit thinner than the Classic Eyebrow. The make-up artist needs to work carefully with the Thin Eyebrow. If made too thin, it may give a harsh or cold look. Or, if the arch is too round, the model may have a surprised or comical look.

Balance the eyebrow with the eye and, overall, the eyebrows to the face. You may find that a combination of two or all three styles is appropriate for the face that you are working on. Not every person will have exact replicas of the styles mentioned. Remember, a well shaped eyebrow will lift and open, while framing the eye.

THE NATURAL EYEBROW

Sharpen an eyebrow pencil to produce a fine point. Follow the illustration of the Natural Eyebrow. Fill in, using the tip of the pencil at a 45 degree angle.

Apply more pressure at the bottom of the stroke, then ease the pressure as the pencil stroke is moved up in a slightly more rounded curve. Placing the pencil next to the skin, start at the bottom of the inner brow, moving upward, drawing in small strokes to look like hair.

Keep the pencil at this angle until the arch has been reached. At the arch, change the angle for each hair stroke. Each stroke is flatter than the one preceding it.

Remember, the Natural Eyebrow is a little fuller and softer looking than the Classic Eyebrow, but it remains within the guidelines of the graph.

The Natural Eyebrow may also be filled in with the wet or dry method previously described using powder eye shadow.

THE THIN EYEBROW

Sharpen the eyebrow pencil often during the application. If the pencil is dull, it will be very difficult to produce a fine line.

Refer to the illustration of the Thin Eyebrow. Fill in

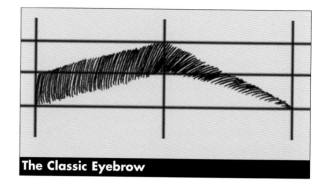
The Classic Eyebrow

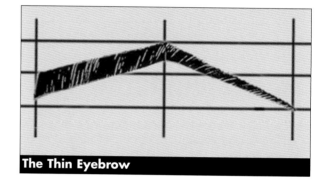
The Thin Eyebrow

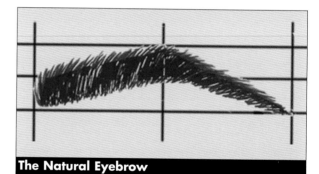
The Natural Eyebrow

using the tip of the pencil at a 45 degree angle. Keep an even amount of pressure on the beginning of the stroke, then ease off the pressure on the end. This will keep the hairs lighter in appearance for the Thin Eyebrow.

Place the pencil next to the skin. Start at the bottom of the inner brow, working upward. Keep the pencil at this angle until the arch has been reached. Then, at the arch change the angle for each hair stroke. Each hair will become flatter than the one preceding it, giving the illusion of real hair.

The Thin Eyebrow is thinner than either the Natural Eyebrow or the Classic Eyebrow. The Thin Eyebrow may also be filled in with the wet/dry method using powder eye shadow. Because the eyebrow is thin, the wet application method works well to keep the hairs defined.

CORRECTING EYEBROW SHAPES

Eyebrow shape can dramatically change one's expression, in a positive or negative way. Eyebrows that are too heavy tend to weigh the face down, while eyebrows that are too sparse leave the eyes somewhat un-framed. Notice how the same face looks very different dependent upon the varying eyebrow shapes.

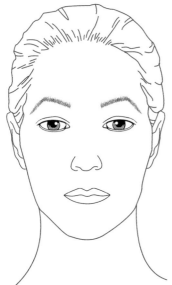

EXAMPLE: Sadness

If the eyebrows are slanting down on the outside edge, the person can have a sad appearance.

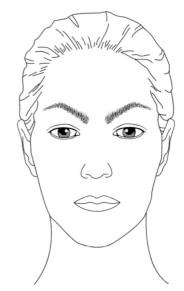

EXAMPLE: Anger

If the brows are slanting down on the inner edge toward the nose, this can be interpreted as angry.

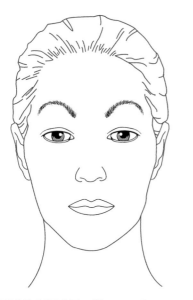

EXAMPLE: Surprise

A very round arch can give one a surprised look.

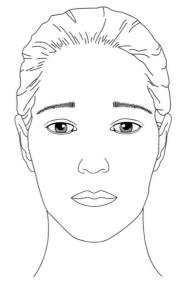

EXAMPLE: Worried/Perplexed

A flat eyebrow can leave one with a worried or perplexed expression.

The following are examples and analysis of eyebrow shapes that need correction.

EXAMPLE: Club Brow

Analysis: The Club Brow is very heavy at the inner brow line, with a club type effect. The arch is somewhat weak, with the rest of the brow too thin and trailing off towards the outer brow line.

EXAMPLE: Dropping Back Brow

Analysis: The Dropping Back Brow starts out fairly well at the inner brow line, but quickly loses strength as the arch drops, taking the rest of the brow with it. By the time the brow ends at the outer brow line, the eye has closed down considerably.

EXAMPLE: Bushy Brow

Analysis: The Bushy Brow is overall too full, wild and generally out of control. It exceeds past the tear duct, closing the space between the eyes. The area between the Upper Lid Line and the bottom of the brow becomes small and heavy.

EXAMPLE: Gapped Brow

Analysis: The Gapped Brow is unkempt, with a few stray hairs and spaces between the hairs.

EXAMPLE: Too Rounded Brow

Analysis: The Too Rounded Brow puts the entire eye out of balance with it's unnatural shape. The arch is far too high. This particular example is also too thin, emphasizing it's roundness even more.

EXAMPLE: Flat Brow

Analysis: The Flat Brow has very little definition, with virtually no arch peak. The width at the inner brow and outer brow are almost the same.

The following corrections are based on the proper positioning for the Classic Eyebrow. It will be up to the make-up artist to actually determine which eyebrow shape is best suited for the individual. The broken lines indicate where corrections need to be done. Corrections can be made by trimming, tweezing, or filling in with eyebrow pencil or eye shadow.

EXAMPLE #1:

The **Club Brow** needs to be trimmed, from the inner brow to the arch peak, then tweezed at the bottom of the inner brow, and filled in to create a defined arch base. Next, fill in and carry through to the outer brow line to create a tapered edge.

Before Correction

Correction

EXAMPLE #2:

The **Dropping Back Brow** needs considerable tweezing to lift the back portion of the eyebrow. Once that has been accomplished, the arch can be filled in to lift and open the eye.

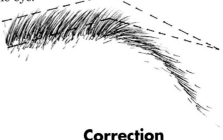

Before Correction

Correction

EXAMPLE #3:

The **Bushy Brow** needs trimming and tweezing. Begin with trimming, then tweeze. It is not necessary to fill in unless there are gaps.

Before Correction

Correction

EXAMPLE #4:

The **Flat Brow** can usually be corrected primarily by filling in and tweezing any stray hairs that may be out of the guidelines of the Classic Brow.

Before Correction

Correction

EXAMPLE #5:

The **Gapped Brow** needs trimming on the top, tweezing a little underneath, and filling in the spaces between the hairs.

Before Correction   **Correction**

EXAMPLE #6:

To bring balance to this **Rounded Brow,** the inner brow will need to be tweezed back to the tear duct, as well as tweezed at the outer brow line. Next, fill in the eyebrow to create a strong arch, then fill in towards the outer brow line.

Before Correction   **Correction**

CHAPTER STUDY QUESTIONS

1. Eyebrows should be the same on everyone ?

2. When tweezing the brow it is important to pull in what direction?

3. What frames the eye?

4. What products may be used to fill in an eyebrow?

5. The arch of the eyebrow consists of what two elements?

6. What tool is used to trim eyebrows?

7. For the classic eyebrow shape, what part of the eye is used to begin laying out the graph?

8. How does eyebrow shape relate to a person's expression?

9. Should eyebrow shapes be customized to fit each person's face?

10. A thin eyebrow works well on someone with what type of face?

CHAPTER 6

EYE SHADOW

Eye Shadow applied properly will enhance the positive features of the eyes, and correct any negative aspects. The make-up artist will learn the differences between Highlight and Shadow and the benefits of each, as it applies to an eye shadow application. The make-up artist will be able to apply eye shadow to draw attention to the eyes. The make-up artist will be able to recognize and correct a variety of problematic areas of the eye. The make-up artist will learn the proper positioning of eye shadow to lift the eye, creating a more youthful look.

PHYSICAL FEATURES OF THE EYE

The space directly above the eye and under the eyebrow is where eye shadow will be placed. This area can vary quite a bit from one person to the next when it comes to width and height. Occasionally, eye shadow will be placed under or around the outer corner of the eye for a more intense or dramatic look.

This area is broken down into the following sections– the upper eye lid, the lower eye lid, the fold, the brow bone, the outer corner, and the tear duct.

On some the skin in this area may be tight, while on others it may be loose. More youthful eyes will have a smooth, taut area in which to apply eye shadow. Mature eyes may have an uneven surface to the upper lid. This is generally referred to as a crepy eye lid.

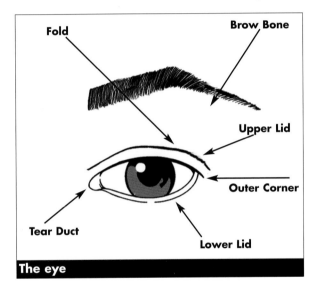

The eye

FOLDS OF THE EYE

There are many different types of eye shapes and eye folds. Eye Shapes can be round or oval, with varying types of folds. The space between the upper lid line and under the brow is the area the artist will concentrate on when applying eye shadow.

The folds are broken down into the following categories: The Flat Eye, the Slight Fold, the Recessed Eye, the Heavy Fold, the Asian Slight Fold and the Asian Heavy Fold. Folds can either be one of or a combination of the above categories.

Placement of eye shadow can either lift up or pull down any of the eye shapes/folds, creating an illusion of something that does not exist. For example you can create the illusion that a heavy fold is more like a slight fold, diminishing the weight of the fold, thereby opening and lifting up the eye.

This in turn creates lift to the entire face and, on a mature person, will create a more youthful look.

The following illustrations show the varying folds that we will be referring to in this chapter. These are general types of folds. Some will have these exact folds while others may have combinations of these folds. The basic principles remain the same when applying eye shadow.

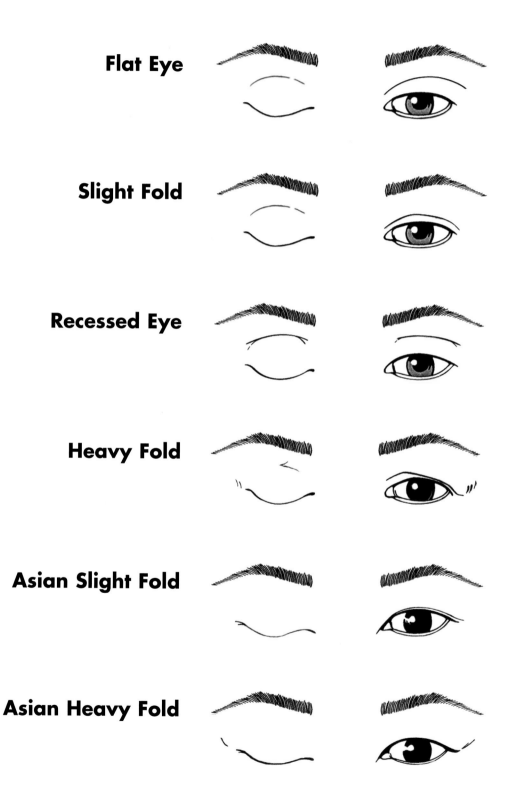

Flat Eye

Slight Fold

Recessed Eye

Heavy Fold

Asian Slight Fold

Asian Heavy Fold

EYE SHADOW PLACEMENT

Eye shadow application is the process used to apply color to the eyes, bringing balance to the eye and ultimately to the face.

Eye shadow is applied after the base and eyebrows have been completed. Allowing the eyes to be framed by the eyebrows helps to determine where product is to be placed. How and where the product is placed is most important, as the technique used can greatly affect the outcome.

SKIN CARE

Skin care is an important factor for a good application of eye shadow. To ensure a smooth eye shadow application, the area above the eye will need to be cleansed and moisturized properly. This can be done along with the individual's regular skin care routine. When this area is ignored, the skin may become dry and rough. Eye shadow applied over rough skin will result in an uneven application, and it will be very difficult, if not impossible, to blend color choices.

BLENDING

Care must be given to the blending of the eye shadow. Blending eye shadow is an art unto itself, as edges should be flawless with an equally smooth transition of colors between where one color begins and another color ends. The proper brush for this powder application will make the difference between an average and a great application. Use one brush for each color choice, and be sure not to mix brushes. Mixing brushes can cause the application to look muddy. Blending is the key to a beautiful eye shadow application.

HIGHLIGHT & SHADOW

Before applying eye shadow, the make-up artist must have an understanding of what eye shadow can do for the eyes.

Highlight and shadow are the two key elements of eye shadow application. Highlight is a much lighter shade of color than shadow. Shadow is deeper or darker in color than highlight. Each has a definite purpose.

Neutral colors, such as warm browns or taupe for shadow, light cream or soft yellow for highlight, work well for all eye colors and most skin tones. Natural looks work best when using neutral shades.

Highlight draws attention to an area by pulling that area forward. Shadow will push an area back, creating depth. Together, this creates balance to an out-of-balance eye, such as an eye that looks tired. The Heavy Fold would be an example of this.

Placement of highlight and shadow on the eye is determined by the type of fold. Each eye fold has its own required needs. By applying the highlight first, a template is left on the eye, indicating where to place shadow.

Each eye fold has its own unique requirements relating to the placement of highlight and shadow; however, there are a few common elements that apply to most folds.

Keep the eye lifted. Eye shadow should not exceed the outer corner of the eye. If the shadow is placed past the corner, the eye will droop, dragging it down. Edges should be well blended to a soft edge. An un-blended edge will appear hard and messy.

The inside edge of shadow (closest to the nose) generally will not exceed below the tear duct. Shadow below the tear duct can also make the eye appear to droop. One exception to this rule is when working with Asian eyes. It may be necessary to go slightly past the tear duct.

The following examples of eye shadow placement are for corrective positions. With some folds there may be more than one choice. Such as is the case with the Asian Folds. There are three different choices for the Asian Slight Fold, each with a unique result. In addition the Asian Heavy Fold may utilize elements taken from the three choices for Asian Slight Fold. Most importantly, remember that highlights pull while shadows push.

Flat Eye

This eye shape is slightly concave, and is called flat because it does not have a fold or tissue that overhangs or is recessed. Lending itself to many different eye shadow treatments, this eye shape is also known as the perfect eye shape, allowing the artist a playground for decorative eye shadow treatments.

Slight Fold

The Slight Fold needs only a minor correction to enhance and open up the eye. Placing highlight on the brow bone and upper lid will give dimension against the shadow.

Recessed Eye

The Recessed Eye generally has little to no fold. Shadow is therefore placed on the area that protrudes from the eye the farthest, usually just below the brow on the bone. Depending on the amount of space available, there is little or no highlight under the eyebrow.

Heavy Fold

The Heavy Fold will need attention paid to the area of the lid where the skin hangs down at its heaviest point. This type of correction can make a tremendous difference in lifting up the eye, creating a more youthfully shaped eye.

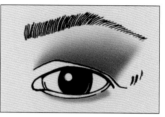

Asian Slight Fold #1

As with most Asian eye shapes, the lid is generally less pronounced, with the fold hanging over the lid in varying degrees. This creates a somewhat flat appearance to the eye. Using highlight and shadow will give the Asian Slight Fold dimension while at the same time creating a more rounded and open look to the eye. This is also known as an imposed caucasian.

Asian Slight Fold #2

This position also works well for this fold, creating dimension in a slightly different area. This will open the eye a little more than the previous position.

Asian Slight Fold #3

With the placement of highlights and shadow this alternative position gives dimension on a slight vertical angle. Notice that the darkest amount of shadow is on the outer and inner portion of the eye.

Asian Heavy Fold

Like the Asian Slight Fold, the Asian Heavy Fold has a flat appearance. The lid is hidden by the heaviness of the fold and, generally, the lashes are pointed down. With highlight and shadow, the heavy fold will become more balanced as well as adding a rounded effect to the eye. It is important to note that all three positions of the Asian Slight Fold will also work on the Asian Heavy Fold.

When reviewing these positions keep in mind that these are corrective positions based on general types of folds that you may be working on. Also it is possible to have combinations of folds. Refer back to the basic principles of highlights, shadows and balance.

The following illustrations show eye shadow placement for the various folds of the open and closed eye. Notice the blending of the shadow into the highlight. This is a soft edge of shadow blending into a soft edge of highlight. Also be aware that the eye shadow does not exceed the outer corner of the eye. When comparing the previous illustration without highlight and shadow on these same folds the difference is quite noticeable. With the right amount of product, in combination with good blending techniques, the eye shadow can appear flawless. Blending is an important aspect of Beauty Make-Up, to be practiced until it is mastered.

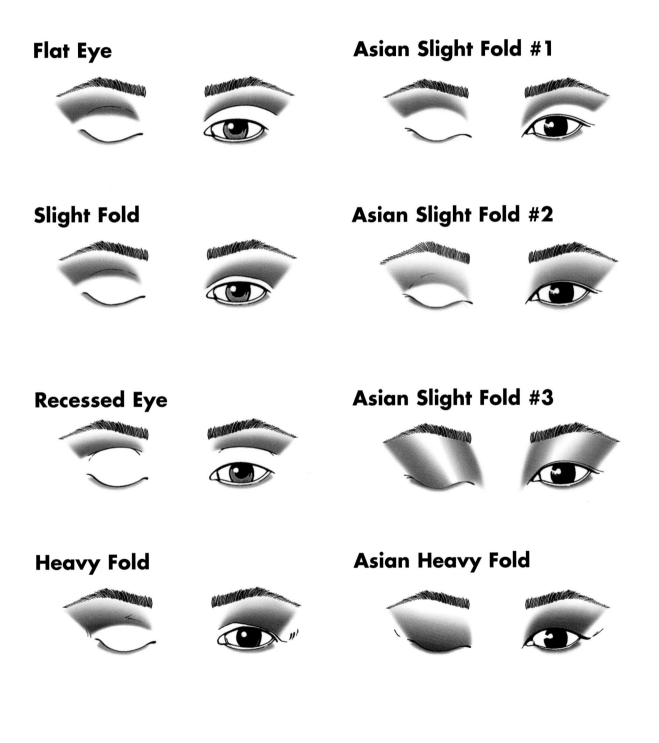

Flat Eye

Asian Slight Fold #1

Slight Fold

Asian Slight Fold #2

Recessed Eye

Asian Slight Fold #3

Heavy Fold

Asian Heavy Fold

Assess the eyes for the shape and type of fold. Not all eyes will be symmetrical. It is possible for one person to have two different folds or to have a variation of the examples of the folds shown. Next, choose a brush to use as the Highlight Brush. A small eye shadow brush works well.

For a natural effect, use a small amount of product on the brush, building up the product on the eye in small increments. This will give the make-up artist control over depth, ensuring an even, well-blended application. Using the product in small increments is recommended so that excess product does not fall from the brush and, ultimately, onto the model's face. This can be a problem when working with dark colors. If eye shadow gets on the model's face the make-up artist will need to remove the excess product and foundation then re-apply foundation before continuing with the eye shadow.

LOADING THE BRUSH

To load the brush, work the product into the brush by lightly tapping the brush into the eye shadow. Load product onto both sides of the brush to evenly distribute the product. Remember to begin with a small amount of product on the brush and build up on the eye, re-loading the brush as needed. Using this technique will allow the artist control over product amount to be applied to the eye. It is much easier to add product when and where it is needed than to have to remove excess product if too much has been applied.

PLACING THE HIGHLIGHT

Following the illustrations provided for each of the folds, place the highlight directly under the eyebrow on the brow bone. With soft, light strokes, or a light tapping motion, place the highlight. Work from the inside corner of the eye, toward the arch of the brow,

stopping at the outside edge of the brow. Blend by using a back and forth stroke of the brush, not lifting it off of the skin. Next, ask the model to close her eyes. Apply highlight to the lid. Work from the inside corner at the tear duct across the middle of the lid, then to the outside corner. Most applications of eye shadow are done from the inside corner to the outside corner. Be careful not to exceed the outside edge, as this will cause the eye to droop. Bring the highlight up to meet the fold. The shadow will be applied next.

PLACING THE SHADOW

Choose a medium-sized eye shadow brush for the shadow portion of the application. Have the model look down. Using a soft, light stroke, or light tapping motion, place the shadow on the fold. Periodically, have the model look straight ahead, so you can check the placement. The deepest or darkest part of the shadow will be placed on the heaviest portion of the fold. Folds generally have a full or drooping effect, so the shadow is used to push that area back. Working up the fold, concentrate on blending the edges from the shadow to the highlight. This is a soft edge to soft edge blending technique.

The make-up artist may choose to place in a drop shadow. A drop shadow will create the illusion that the lower lashes are thick enough to cast a shadow. On occasion this is done simply to balance out a heavy upper eye treatment. The Drop Shadow is placed on the lower lid, a delicate area of the eye, under the lower lashes. Have the model look up while applying. Use a small eye shadow brush or an angle/wedge shaped brush. With light gentle strokes place the shadow color on the lower lid. Blend evenly across the lower lid. Have the model look straight ahead. Look into the mirror to check the work. Adjust as necessary.

FASHION AND GLAMOUR

Most often the make-up artist will work with neutral tones for natural or clean beauty looks. However, within these neutral tones, there are numerous techniques that can add variety. These techniques will allow the make-up artist to elaborate on a natural application, creating a dramatic look for a more glamourous eye make-up treatment.

The shade of the shadows chosen are equally as important to a well-blended application. Neutral eye shadow shades can range from pale yellow to black. How these are applied can change and enhance the eyes.

The effect an artist can achieve is based on not only the shade chosen, but how the shadow is layered and blended. The make-up artist may choose to use several shades of shadow. When this is the case, the shadow is applied according to the shade, layering on the shadow from the lightest shade to the darkest. This is a building-up process, giving the make-up artist complete control over the dimension of the final look.

For example, adding a deeper shade along the fold will give the illusion of depth. This method will also make the color of the iris seem more vibrant, drawing attention to the eyes.

Generally, for a fashion eye shadow treatment, the shadow will connect with the drop shadow at the outer corner. An example of this is what is known as a smokey eye.

Also a consideration in choosing a matte or iridescent color. Once again this is dependent upon the desired look.

NOTE:

When doing a heavier eye shadow treatment, it is advisable to place a colorless loose powder on the areas directly under the eyes to catch any possible fallout from the shadows, particularly when working with dark colors. This will help to prevent damage to the base and/or corrective application. Once the eyes are complete, the loose powder is then brushed away, leaving the base clean and debris free.

These examples show several of the different looks that may be created by adding layers of shadow, working from the lightest shade of shadow to the darkest. Each look progressively becomes more dramatic. Any one of these looks may be used depending on the desired look.

EXAMPLE 1

This eye shadow treatment is the standard shadow positioning for the flat eye. It is also the base from which the other shadow treatments begin. Highlight is placed under the eyebrow and on the lid, then a taupe shadow is placed as shown.

EXAMPLE 2

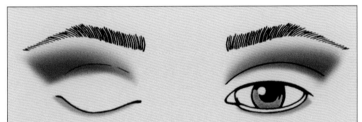

With this eye shadow treatment, the shadow has been brought down slightly onto the lid, narrowing the lid space. Starting with a taupe shade and adding a slightly darker color such as a deep brown at this point will give extra depth to the eye . Highlight is on the lid and brow bone.

EXAMPLE 3

This eye shadow treatment goes around the outside of the eye. After the highlight is applied, layer in shades of taupe and deep brown. The darker shades should be at the fold, blending up into the lighter shadow color.

EXAMPLE 4

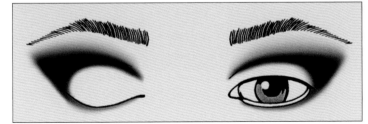

This eye shadow treatment is similar to the above look except that black has been added on top of the deep brown and once again blended up. When working with black shadows, be careful not to have too much product on the brush.

EYE SHADOW TRENDS

Trendy is whatever the market will bear for the times. Some years the trends may be soft, natural or subtle, the next year the trend could be bright red with purple on the eyes. Whatever it might be, the make-up artist must be ready and willing to experiment and have fun with the ever changing looks.

There are an endless variety of eye shadow treatments. One can look at the eyes as a playground, with the looks achieved limited only by the make-up artist's imagination. Color choices are vast, with combinations ranging from subtle to wild, matte to iridescent, light to dark, and warm to cool. Mixing and matching in all forms is what is seen in today's make-up. Eye shadows are more vibrant than ever, with varying shades of the brightest yellows and oranges, purples and electric blues in most pallets.

There are several rules that apply no matter what look is to be achieved–

- **Highlights pull, shadows push.**

- **Matte colors tend to absorb light.**

- **Iridescent colors reflect light.**

- **Build and layer the eye shadow in small increments.**

- **Blend, Blend, Blend....**

Arranging the Eye Shadow Color palette into groups allows the make-up artist to see the colors in their true shades. Example, place together all colors that are likely to be used as highlight, such as shades of vanilla, bone or pale yellow. Place together all the neutral tones used for natural or daytime looks, including light browns, taupes, warm browns, deep browns and black. Have another section in the palette for metallic or iridescent colors, including golds, coppers, and silver. Greens should be grouped together, matte and iridescent alike. Blues, purples, pinks, and plums should also have a section in the artist's pallet.

Using the same positioning guidelines for the different folds, try these color combinations, layering the product from light to dark.

Color Combination 1:
Light shade of pink for highlight, placed on the lid and under the brow. A medium shade of plum as shadow.

Color Combination 2:
A soft cream color as the highlight for the brow bone, with a soft apricot as the highlight for the lid. A medium reddish brown at the fold for shadow.

Color Combination 3:
A metallic golden yellow as the highlight for the lid, metallic lime green for the fold, and a cream color as the highlight for the brow bone.

Color Combination 4:
A muted earthy green on the lid, iridescent deep purple for the fold, and a cream color as the highlight for the brow bone.

Color Combination 5:
A metallic deep aqua on the lid, metallic purple/blue for the fold, and a light shade of soft pink as the highlight for the brow bone.

For drop shadows, try any of the colors that were used on the folds.

CHAPTER STUDY QUESTIONS

1. What do highlights do in an eye shadow treatment ?

2. The eye shadow treatment is built up from?

3. Drop shadows have what type of an edge?

4. Do matte colors absorb or reflect light?

5. Iridescent colors absorb or reflect light?

6. On a heavy fold where is the darkest part of the shadow placed?

7. Proper skin care can enhance an eye shadow application?

8. Blending is not necessary in an eye shadow application?

9. A drop shadow may be used to create the illusion of what?

10. One can look at the eyes as what?

CHAPTER 7
EYE LINER

Eyeliner that is flawlessly applied will enhance any make-up application. The make-up artist will learn the skills to achieve various styles of Eye Liner using several types of product. The artist will be able to apply a variety of Eye Liner positions. The artist will learn to apply these Eye Liner positions using Cake Eye Liner, Pencil and Powder Eye Shadow.

PHYSICAL FEATURES OF THE EYE AS IT RELATES TO EYE LINER APPLICATION

As previously described in the Eye Shadow Chapter, there are several parts of the eye that are involved with the application of make-up. With the application of eye liner, the primary areas are the upper and lower lids.

Other parts that are affected are the outer corner, the tear duct and in some cases the fold. Working with eye liner involves working closely with the inside corner at the tear duct, a very delicate area that must be regarded with caution.

The illustration on this page shows the parts of the eye which can also be viewed in the eye shadow chapter.

EYE LINER PLACEMENT

Eye liner is a critical portion of the eye make-up application. At this point, several other eye treatments have been done: foundation, eyebrows, and eye shadow.

Eye liner brings the eye make-up together by defining the eye. Placement of the eye liner begins at the tear duct of the upper lid, across the center of the lid and down to the outside corner of the eye.

It is very important that the eye liner does not exceed the outside corner. Eye liner that exceeds this will cause the eye to droop down. Equally as important is the smoothness and thickness of the application. Consistency in both are required for an even eye liner application.

EYE LINER APPLICATION

Eye liner application is the procedure used to place an eye liner product on the eye lids. Eye liner enhances the make-up application by defining the eye. Applied after eye shadow and before mascara, eye liner is an intricate part of the make-up process.

As in most make-up choices, the product used is dependent upon the look to be achieved and the model's eye type. An eye liner application can be thick or thin, hard edged or soft edged. The choice and control is up to the make-up artist. Products used vary from a powder application using eye shadow to an application achieved using a cake eyeliner.

Eye liner is generally applied to the upper lid of the eye, next to the lashes. Some eye liner positions require eye liner to be applied to the lower lid. In some instances, the fold can be a factor in the application of eye liner.

It is important to strive for a clean, even application of eye liner. An even application is smooth across the lid and balanced eye to eye. Eye liner positions can be used to create illusions, making wide-set eyes seem closer together, or narrow set eyes further apart.

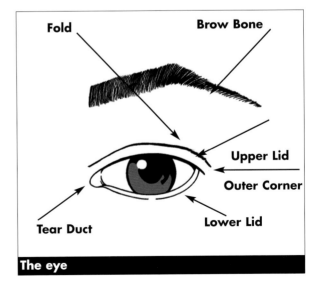

Fold **Brow Bone** **Upper Lid** **Outer Corner** **Lower Lid** **Tear Duct**

The eye

STRAIGHT EYE LINER

Straight Eye Liner application requires a few technical steps and a steady hand. This position is used primarily to define the eye. Straight Eye Liner follows the contour or the curve of the eye, hugging the lashes. Applied to the upper lid, its thinnest point begins at the tear duct. From the center of the lid to the outer corner it maintains the same thickness. With cake, or powder eye liner, the application method is the same. The differences are in the preparation of the product and the final look.

Eye liner is applied to the eye with the eye open, not closed. With the eye closed, the skin may be pulled too tightly. When the eye is open the eye liner will not be smooth or even. Do not pull the eye lid up as this will distort the shape of the eye, creating an application that is uneven. If it is necessary to pull the lid taut, do so by lifting above the brow.

The model will look down during application. When applying eye liner to the inside corner at the tear duct, the model will look in the opposite direction toward the outer corner. When applying eye liner to the outer corner, the model will look in toward the tear duct. This will keep the lid taut and accessible.

Cake Eye Liner Application:

A cake eye liner application produces a hard, defined edge that is solid in color. When dry, this application will have a lasting quality.

• When using a cake eye liner it is first necessary to make a slurry. A slurry is made by wetting the eye liner brush with water and rolling it into the cake eye liner. The consistency of the cake eye liner is important in achieving an even application. Too wet and the product is not solid in color and is likely to run on the eye lid. Too dry and the product will skip, leaving gaps in the application. Testing on the back of your hand before applying to the eye lid is recommended.

• When applying, do not point the end of the brush straight into the lid. The make-up artist will have more control over the application when laying the brush flat against the lashes. The amount of pressure placed on the brush will determine how thick or how thin the eye liner application will be. More pressure creates a thicker liner, less pressure creates a thinner liner.

• Have the model look down to the outer corner of the eye. Lay the point of the brush flat against the upper lid next to the lashes at the tear duct. The end of the brush should be pointed in toward the tear duct.

• Use a dragging motion to pull the brush to the center of the upper lid; keep an even amount of

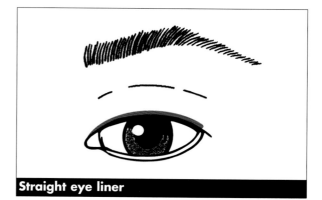

Straight eye liner

pressure on the brush. Once the center of the lid has been reached, lift the brush away from the lid. Reload the brush.

• Have the model look toward the tear duct. Turn the brush so that it is now pointed toward the outside corner. Place the brush flat against the lashes at the outside corner and drag the brush up to the center of the lid, meeting the existing liner. There should be no breaks or bumps where the two strokes meet. This should appear to be one even line hugging the lashes.

Eye liner application is best done in fluid, consistent strokes. The fewer strokes the better, with most applications being done in only two strokes.

Powder Application:

Eye shadows may be used as eye liner. They may be applied dry or wet. For both applications, a small angle or wedge brush works well, giving a fine controlled stroke.

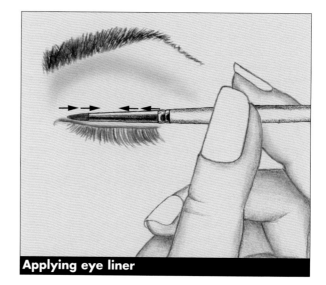

Applying eye liner

Dry Application:

Press the edge of the angle or wedge brush into the eye shadow and tap. Be sure to evenly coat both sides of the brush. Do not overload the brush. It is better to use small amounts and reload the brush as necessary. A dry application will give a soft edge to the eye liner.

• After loading the brush, have the model look down to the outer corner, and apply to the inside at the tear duct. With a dry powder application, it is best to tap on the product in small increments across the upper lid next to the lashes.

• Work from the tear duct up to the center of the lid. Reload the brush, have the model look to the inside, turn the brush over, and apply from the outer corner to the center of the lid. When using a dragging motion,the powder could fall from the Upper Lid, creating problems that will need to be addressed. When powder falls onto the face it can become mixed into the foundation that has been applied previously. The artist will need to remove the foundation in this area, then re-apply. Putting a tissue under the lashes while using a powder product on the eyes is a good way to prevent this unnecessary additional step.

Wet Application:

Dampen the brush in water, press the edge of the brush into the product and work it in a back and forth motion to evenly coat both sides of the brush. Be careful not to get the brush too wet. A good test is to use the back of your hand to see how opaque the product looks. If it is not consistent in color, it may be too wet. If it skips as it is applied, it may be too dry. It is better to use small amounts and reload the brush as necessary.

• Have the model look down and toward the outer corner. Place the angle/wedge brush at the tear duct. With the angled part of the brush flat against the upper lid next to the lashes, drag up to the center of the lid.

• If necessary reload the brush. Turn the brush over. With the model looking toward the tear duct place the brush at the outer corner and drag to the center. Eye liner should be smooth, with no bumps where the two strokes meet.

Pencil Application:

An eye liner pencil will need to be sharpened with a make-up pencil sharpener before each use. The pencil can be used as is, applied directly to the eye. Most eye liner pencils can produce either a sharp hard edge or, when smudged, a soft edge.

• To produce an even smooth application, place the pencil at a 45-degree angle. Do not point the end of the pencil straight onto the upper lid. This will cause skips in the application.

• Have the model look down to the outer corner. Begin at the tear duct and lightly drag the pencil up to the center of the upper lid.

• Have the model look toward the tear duct. Turn pencil so that the end of it is now toward the outer corner. Apply from the outer corner up to the center, dragging the pencil lightly across the upper lid to meet the existing liner.

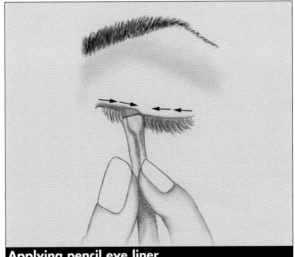

Applying pencil eye liner

Cylinder with highlights and shadow

CORRECTIVE EYE LINER

In addition to Straight Eye Liner there are three primary corrective eye liner positions. (These are the foundation of all eye liner positions.) They are the Natural, Fashion and Glamour Eye Liner positions.

Corrective positions each have a unique task with a common effect of lifting the eye. Optical lift is done by keeping the liner above an imaginary line that runs horizontally through the center of the eye. Any liner placed below this line will drop the eye down, creating a drooping effect. This is rarely if ever flattering to the model.

One common element among these eye liner positions is their ability to lift the eyes.

NOTE:
Rest your pinky finger on the model's cheek to steady your hand. This will help you produce a smooth eye liner application.

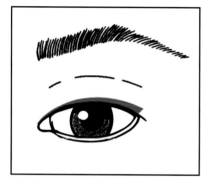

NATURAL EYE LINER
This liner position is in the general shape of a wedge or inclined plane. The function of an inclined plane is to lift one object to another. The thin end of the liner begins at the tear duct and ends at, but does not exceed, the outer corner. This liner position gradually gets thicker as it proceeds to the center. At the outer corner the liner is at it's thickest point. It's distinguishing characteristic is it's wedge shape.

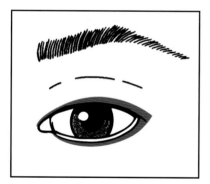

FASHION EYE LINER
This second corrective position has a bottom liner that comes up to meet the top liner. Notice the Fashion Liner position also uses the optical inclined plane effect by connecting above the horizontal center of the eye. The Fashion Eye Liner's distinguishing characteristic is that the outer corner is closed. The liner on the upper lid begins thin at the tear duct and progressively get thicker as it moves toward the outer corner. The liner on the bottom does the same, with less thickness overall. The Fashion Eye Liner's inherent effect is that it will make narrow-set eyes seem further apart.

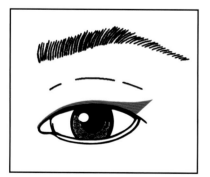

GLAMOUR EYE LINER
This third corrective position's distinguishing characteristic is that the eye liner treatment is wide open. Liner on the upper lid begins thin at the tear duct and stays thin as it follows the contour of the eye. It drops slightly just before it lifts up. The outer corner of the upper liner is slightly recessed and has a sharp angular lift. The Glamour Eye Liner's inherent effect is that it will make wide-set eyes seem closer together.

CORRECTIVE EYE LINER APPLICATION

Just as each eye liner position is unique in appearance, so is the application to achieve it. The following describes the application for each position.

NATURAL EYE LINER

Refer to the illustration for Natural Eye Liner.

For the Natural Eye Liner position, begin as if applying Straight Eye Liner. With the Straight Eye Liner the outer corner will be built up to achieve the wedge of the Natural Eye Liner position. Keep in mind the top part of the wedge stops at the outer corner.

Application: With the model looking toward the outer corner:

• Lay the brush flat, with the pointed end in at the tear duct. Drag the brush up to the center of the lid. Lift the brush off the lid.

• Turn the brush in the opposite direction. Have the model look down toward the tear duct. From the outer corner drag the brush up to the center. The model is still looking toward the tear duct. Repeat.

• Lay the brush flat on top of the liner already placed on the upper lid. Apply a little pressure to the brush to get more thickness from the line. Drag the brush straight to the center of the upper lid and stop.

• When the eye is open, looking straight ahead, the liner will have the same curve as the eye. Have the model look up straight ahead so you can check for positioning. This may take one or two strokes in thickness to build up properly. If the brush is placed correctly, the wedge will develop.

FASHION EYE LINER

Refer to the illustration for Fashion Eye Liner.

To create the Fashion Eye Liner, the upper lid begins with the Straight Eye Liner position. Before the thickness builds on the upper lid, the lower lid position will be addressed. This will allow a reference point for the liner position for the upper lid.

Application: With the model looking toward the outer corner:

Upper Lid:
• Lay the brush flat, with the pointed end in at the tear duct on the upper lid. Drag the brush up to the center of the lid. Lift the brush off the lid. Turn the brush in the opposite direction.

• Have the model look down toward the tear duct. From the outer corner, drag the brush up to the center.

Lower Lid:
• Have the model look straight ahead. Envision an imaginary line running horizontally through the center of the eye. With the eye liner brush, place a small dot on the Upper Lid where the upper and lower liners will connect. This is above the non-existent line. The eye liner will not exceed this point.

• Reload the eye liner brush. Have the model look up to the inside corner of the eye. Lay the brush flat on the dot with the pointed tip directed to the outside, on the lower lid. Drag the brush down from the dot along the lower lid. Ease off the pressure while dragging the brush to create a thinner line toward the center. The connection of the two strokes should be smooth and consistent.

Upper Lid:
• Have the model look down toward the tear duct. Laying the brush flat at the dot, drag the eye liner brush to the center of the upper lid. This step may need to be repeated until this area is filled in. Have the model look straight ahead to check the positioning. Adjust as necessary.

GLAMOUR EYE LINER

For the Glamour Eye Liner position, keep in mind the openness of this position. It is a the only Eye Liner position of the three corrective positions that does not start with the Straight Eye Liner application. It has a unique look as it slopes and then lifts up.

Application: Refer to the illustration for Glamour Eye Liner.

• Have the model look down toward the Outer Corner. Lay the brush flat, pointed end in at the Tear Duct. Drag the brush up to the center of the lid, keeping the liner very thin, with the brush closely hugging the lashes. Lift the brush off the lid.

• Have the model look straight ahead. Place a dot on the outer corner where this Upper Liner is to end. Turn the brush. Point the tip of brush to the outer corner. Drag the brush toward the center, still hugging the lashes closely.

• Have the model look straight ahead. Return brush to the beginning point at the dot. Drag the brush down and toward the center, to fill in, creating the wing of the Glamour eye.

ADJUSTING LINER FOR DIFFICULT FOLDS

Part of being a make-up artist requires that the artist be able to create illusion.

Such is the case with some folds that require adjustment. These folds do not always fit in the general application process and may need to be adapted on an individual basis. Not every person will have the exact type of fold as the examples. Some may have combinations of the varying folds. Not all eye liner positions will work for every one of the folds.

Adjustments are made based on the amount of eye lid space the make-up artist has to work with. Often the Asian Slight Fold and most certainly the Asian Heavy Fold may need an adjusted technique to create the illusion of a Straight Eye Liner application.

The Asian Slight Fold, the Asian Heavy Fold and the Heavy Fold do not lend themselves graciously to the necessary positioning of the Fashion Eye Liner and the Glamour Eye Liner. Due to the drooping action of these eye folds, there often is not enough eye lid space. These positions on some eyes can be difficult to achieve and, on occasion, even impossible. One possibility is to use eye color instead of liner, treating it more like a shadow position with the feel of a Fashion or Glamour Liner position.

The following illustrations show a method used to adjust Straight Eye Liner for the Asian Slight Fold and the Asian Heavy Fold. These same techniques may be used in adapting a liner position for the Heavy Fold.

Remember, the make-up artist creates the illusion of something that does not exist. Not all folds will work with all techniques, and adjustments are often necessary.

This illustration shows the steps needed for the Asian Slight Fold and the Asian Heavy Fold in order to produce a Straight Eye Liner application.

Asian Slight Fold

STEP 1:
Have the model look forward to locate where the fold is. On the fold, place dots to create a template for placement of the eye liner. **STEP 2:** With the eye closed, the artist will be able to see the template. Note: the line begins at the tear duct and moves to the outer corner of the eye, not where the fold ends.

STEP 3:
Following the dotted line, fill in with product to the lash line, making sure the upper lid is well covered.
STEP 4:
When the eye is open this application produces a Straight Eye Liner position, defining the eye.

Asian Heavy Fold

STEP 1:
Have the model look forward to locate the fold. It will be very close to the lash line. On the fold place dots to create a template for the placement of the eye liner. **STEP 2:** With the eye closed, the artist will be able to see the template. Note: the line begins at the tear duct and moves to the outer corner of the eye, not where the fold ends.

STEP 3:
Following the same technique as the Asian Slight Fold, fill in with product from the dotted line to the lash line. Be sure the upper lid is well covered. **STEP 4:** When the eye is open, this application produces a Straight Eye Liner position, defining the eye. If the Eye Liner exceeds the outer corner the eye will droop.

When an eye has a difficult fold, the make-up artist can make that fold work to an advantage.

EXAMPLE
The Asian Slight Fold and The Asian Heavy Fold with Straight Eye Liner

These folds can be so heavy that the upper lid is not exposed and lashes point straight down. When applying a Straight Eye Liner, generally the liner is applied to the space of the upper lid. To create the effect of a Straight Eye Liner the make-up artist uses illusion.

Application: Use a cake eye liner or a wet application of eye shadow with an angle/wedge brush. Have the model look forward. This allows the artist to determine the location or position of the fold.

• With the model looking forward, create a dotted line across the edge of the fold with one of the chosen liner products. This line will be the template for placement of the eye liner product.

• Using very small dots begin the line at the tear duct and stop at the outer corner. The fold will exceed the outer corner, but it is important to stop the eye liner at the outer corner.

• Once the dotted line is placed, have the model close her eyes. Fill in with eye liner from the dotted line, all the way to the lash line. Allow the liner to dry before opening the eyes. When the eyes are closed this will look like excess eye liner; however, with the eyes open it will appear as a Straight Eye Liner application.

EXAMPLE
The Heavy Fold with Fashion Eye Liner

This fold is at its heaviest where it is most critical to the connection of the Fashion Eye Liner position. Because of this, generally, liquid liners with hard edges do not work well. A possible solution would be to use a dry powder application of eye shadow. Powders have a softer edge to them. With this treatment the eye color creates soft edges that will help to diminish the heaviness of the fold. The effect is a combination of an eye liner shape with eye color transition of dark to light.

Application: This application is similar to the eye shadow treatment used to create the illusion of an eye liner application. Use eye shadow dry.

• Have the model look forward. With the angle/wedge brush, draw in a solid line where the product is to be placed, warm brown being a good color choice; it is dark enough to see where the product is placed and not too dark in the event any adjustments need to be made. Use very little product and build as necessary.

• With the model looking down, fill in to the lash line. Check the work as the model looks forward.

• Place the warm brown on the lower lid to meet the outer corner of the upper lid application. Recall the imaginary horizontal line that runs through the eye.

Remember, the Fashion Eye Liner connects above this line.

• With a darker shade of brown, apply to the upper lid at the lash line. Work the edge into the warm brown. Repeat on the lower lid. Less product, instead of more with blended edges, will keep this eye from looking overdone.

NOTE: Use small, fine dotted lines when working with heavier folds.

EYE LINER VARIATIONS

• With slight adjustments eye liner treatments can create a variety of looks. Hard or soft edges (refer to the Corrective Make-Up chapter) are elements that can change the appearance of eye liner. Both can be adapted to eye liner applied to the upper lid and the lower lid.

• The use of a drop shadow will also change the eye liner treatment. A drop shadow is a soft edged liner applied to the lower lid, creating the illusion of a shadow being cast by the lower lashes.

• Layering two or more eye liners on top of each other is an interesting way to create variety within the

eye make-up treatment.

• Combining hard edges with soft edges is an innovative way to create dimension within the eye liner.

• Using different colors can broaden the spectrum of eye liner treatments. Combine colors, hard/soft edges and layering for an endless array of looks.

The following illustrations are examples of the variations.

Hard Edge-Straight Eye Liner with a Drop Shadow

Hard Edge-Natural Eye Liner with a Drop Shadow

Hard Edge-Glamour Eye Liner with a Drop Shadow

Soft Edge-Straight Eye Liner

Soft Edge-Natural Eye Liner

Soft Edge-Fashion Eye Liner

Soft Edge-Glamour Eye Liner

EXAMPLE: Hard Edges

Hard edges are those created with cake liner, or a wet application of eye shadow.

Application: Apply, as previously described in the Eye Liner Application section, and allow to dry.

EXAMPLE: Soft Edges using Dry Application

Soft edges, are those created by a dry application of eye shadow.

Application: Apply as previously described in the Eye Liner Application section.

EXAMPLE Soft Edges

In this case soft edges are created by smudging out the hard edges of a wet application of eye shadow.

Application:

Apply, as previously described in the Eye Liner Application section. When dry, dampen a clean, small angle/wedge brush. Remove excess water on the back of the hand. With the edge of the brush, gently go over the top edge only with a back and forth motion until the top of the hard edge is smudged. Be careful not to get the brush too wet. Excessive moisture will lift more product than necessary. Too little moisture on the brush will cause the product to flake.

EXAMPLE: Soft Edges using a dry angle/wedge brush. Soft edges can be created when using a dry angle/wedge brush with a pencil eye liner.

Application:

Apply, as previously described in the eye liner application section.

With the dry brush, gently go over the liner using short, light strokes to create a smoked effect.

EXAMPLE: Drop Shadow

A drop shadow is always a soft edge, creating the illusion of thick lower lashes. This may be the most common variation of eye liner treatments. It is often used to balance a heavy upper eye make-up treatment.

Application:

Any of the methods described in the Eye Liner Application section for soft edges will work for drop shadows.

EXAMPLE: Layering Eye Liner (Wet and/or Dry)

Layering eye liner can be accomplished using a lighter color liner underneath a darker liner.

Application:

Apply a medium warm brown liner to the lid first. When dry, apply a thinner liner of black on top.

EXAMPLE: Combining Hard/Soft Edges

Combining hard edges with soft edges is an interesting way to create dimension within the eye liner.

Application:

Lay down a soft edge of dark brown, with a hard edge of black over the dark brown.

EXAMPLE: Combining Several Elements

Using different colors can open the spectrum of eye liner treatment to new heights. Combine colors, hard/soft edges and layering for an endless array of looks.

Application:

There are numerous selections available for this eye liner treatment, the only limitation being the lack of imagination.

CHAPTER STUDY QUESTIONS

1. What does eye liner do for the eye?

2. What corrective eye liner position visually corrects wide-set eyes?

3. Which eye liner position corrects at the outside corner of the eye?

4. Should every make-up require eye liner?

5. Which eye liner position is not a corrective position?

6. Which eye liner position visually corrects narrow-set eyes?

7. Can eye shadow be used as eye liner?

8. When applying eye liner to the inside corner, which direction should the model look?

9. Should cake liner be used wet or dry?

10. Do all eye liner positions have a hard edge?

CHAPTER 8
EYE LASHES

The objective of this chapter is to develop the proper skills for curling the lashes, as well as the application of Mascara. The make-up artist will learn the techniques used to enhance the Eye Lashes, drawing attention to the eyes. This includes the use and application of False Eye Lashes. It is the final step of the eye treatment in a make-up application.

PHYSICAL FEATURES OF THE EYE LASHES

Eye lashes are the hairs that grow from the upper and lower lids. It is believed that the eye lashes protect the eyes from small amounts of falling debris. The lashes on the upper lid grow upward in a curve from the lid. The lashes on the lower lid grow downward in a curve.

Eye lashes can be thick, thin, curly or straight and come in a variety of colors.

Women have been striving for years to have long, thick and, usually, dark eye lashes. Eye lashes, regardless of whether they are natural or enhanced with an eye lash curler and mascara, will further enhance eye make-up, creating a finished look. When mascara alone is not enough, false lashes can be of great benefit in giving a dramatic look to the eye.

ANALYZING THE EYE LASHES

Analyze the lashes by looking at the model and asking the following questions:

Are the lashes curly?
Are the lashes straight?
What color are the lashes?
How thick or thin are the lashes?
Are the lashes difficult to see?

CURLING THE LASHES
Curling eye lashes will give a flattering curve to the upper lashes and create the illusion that the lashes are actually longer than they are. Curved lashes can be seen more clearly against the background of the fold. Adding an application of mascara will make the lashes appear thicker and more visible. Curling is generally done only on the upper lashes.

HOW TO CURL LASHES WITH AN EYE LASH CURLER
• Use an eye lash curler with the model looking straight ahead. Have the model look down slightly and hold her head still.

• Place the eye lash curler at the base of the upper lid, capturing the upper lashes in the eye lash curler. Squeeze down gently on the lashes, being careful not to pull on them. Hold for a few seconds and release. Do not remove the eye lash curler.

• This action will be repeated several times as the artist moves upward toward the ends of the lashes; this is called walking, and will prevent a dent to the lashes while keeping the curve consistent.

HOW TO CURL LASHES WITH A SPOON
• Another method used to curl lashes may be done with a spoon. An ordinary metal teaspoon from any cutlery drawer (not a measuring teaspoon) will do nicely.

• Placing the lashes between the thumb (on the bottom) and the spoon (on the top), gently move the spoon over the thumb. This will have the same effect as curling a ribbon. The more this is done the more curl may be achieved.

MASCARA
There are two types of Mascara most frequently used. The first is a Cream Mascara. Most often this product will come packaged in a tube with an applicator wand. The second is a Cake Mascara, requiring water to activate this solid product.

If thickening or lengthening the lashes is the desired effect, cream mascara works best. When only coloring the lashes is desired, cake mascara works well. This is also the method used most often on men..

CREAM MASCARA APPLICATION
• Applying a cream mascara can be done directly from the tube only when this is not a shared tube. It is recommended that each model have a personally owned tube of mascara. When working with several actors/models at a time, it is good practice to put the individual's name on the tube. This will prevent mixing up tubes or someone else's mascara.

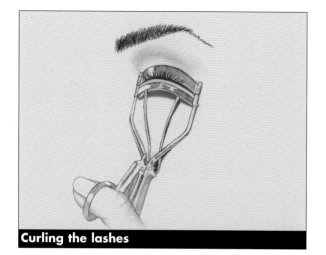

Curling the lashes

• The use of a disposable mascara wand is recommended. When using the disposable mascara wands, it is advisable to remove mascara with the applicator wand then place mascara on a palette. From the palette the mascara can be placed on the disposable wand. Do not put a disposable wand into the tube more than once. This is very unsanitary and can cause bacterial problems to the eye.

• When the mascara is on the wand, have the model look halfway down.

• Holding the wand horizontally, begin applying mascara to the top of the upper lashes, working from the base of the lashes out to the ends. Apply evenly from the tear duct to the outer corner.

• Have the model look up slightly and apply mascara from underneath the upper lashes, working from the base of the lashes to the tips.

• Re-load the mascara wand from the palette or personal mascara tube. Apply mascara to the lower lashes, working from the base to the tips.

Check for an even application of mascara without any clumps. If thicker lashes are desired, apply a second coat of mascara.

If clumping occurs, the use of a metal eye lash comb will remove additional unwanted mascara.

Applying cream mascara to the lashes

CAKE MASCARA APPLICATION

• Applying cake mascara is done with the use of either a small fan brush or a disposable mascara wand.

• Water in a spray bottle is needed to moisten the cake mascara before it will transfer to either applicator. When using the fan brush, be sure to coat both sides of the brush by stroking it across the product in one direction and then reversing the motion. This will help to produce an even application of mascara to the lashes.

• When using a disposable mascara wand, rotating the wand by rolling it through the product will coat all sides of this round brush.

• To keep the product sanitary, it is recommended you spray the cake mascara with a light coat of 99%

Cake mascara applied with a fan brush

alcohol after each use. Doing this after each use will allow the product to dry completely between uses.

• Start on the upper eye lashes with the model looking down. Apply the cake mascara on the top side of the lashes. Next, have the model look up, then continue the application by working from the base of the eye lashes to the ends. When finished, both sides of the upper lashes should have an even coat of cake mascara.

• Re-load the fan brush. Next, place a tissue under the lower lashes. This will help during application, and will prevent mascara from getting on the skin.

COLOR CHOICES

Today there are many color choices for mascara, ranging from rich colors such as eggplant to the brightest blues and even yellows.

For a natural look, browns and blacks would be the colors of choice. For lighter skin tones, choose brown. For darker skin tones, choose black mascara.

Ultimately, it is up to the make-up artist to choose the best color for the desired result.

FALSE EYE LASHES

False eyelashes are an accessory used by make-up artists to temporarily enhance the lash lines of actors and models. They are available in a wide variety of lengths, thicknesses, and colors; false eyelashes are made from synthetic or natural hair; ranging in price based on the quality of the lashes.

False lashes can appear to be completely natural to very dramatic. They come in a variety of styles and are commonly referred to as Strips, Individuals and Singles. No matter what the style, all lashes are glued in place.

STRIP LASHES

Eyelash hairs are glued into a strip that follows the shape of one's natural lash line, extending from the inner corner of the eyelash to the outer corner. Strips are made for both upper and lower lash lines (lowers are commonly referred to as unders on the package). The strip may vary in thickness from light to heavy depending upon the thickness of the lashes it must support.

INDIVIDUAL LASHES

These lashes are known by several different names, with individuals, clumps and flares being their common ones. Several lashes are grouped together and set into a "bead" of plastic at one end, to hold them together. Individual lashes can look very natural, almost indiscernible on the lash line; they are customarily used on the upper lash line, but can also be used on the lower lash line. They are generally lighter in weight than strip lashes and may be more comfortable to the wearer.

SINGLE LASHES

As the name implies, single lashes are one to two strands of hair. These can be used on the upper lid and lower lid, but their primary function is to fill in spaces along the lash line.

REMOVAL AND POSITIONING

False eyelashes are packaged in a plastic container called the bed; strip lashes are packaged in pairs. There is a right side and a left side, to be placed on each respective lash line.

To remove a strip lash and maintain the lashes shape (curve), place your thumb at the top of the lash bed (the base of the strip) and gently roll your thumb downward, keeping the shape of the lash base intact, as you release the lash from the lash bed.

To remove individuals and singles from their packaging, tweezers may be used. Take your tweezer and slide one side under the hairs, getting as close to the base of the lash(es) as possible. Gently close the tweezer and lift the lash out of the bed. If you grab the tips of the lashes, the hairs will often splay and you won't be able to use the affected lash; bending the bed

into an arch helps to lift the lash up from the bed, making the lash(es) easier to grab.

Lashes are placed onto the lash line with eyelash adhesive, of which their are many manufactures. A standard good eyelash adhesive goes on white, turns clear when it is dry, and is waterproof, however you may prefer to use a dark glue when doing a heavy eye treatment.

False eyelashes are already curled and flared, so it is not necessary to curl them with an eyelash curler once they have been applied to the eye. However, if the artist wants to curl them manually, it is best to do so before they have been applied (eliminating the risk of pulling them off of the eye). It is recommended that the artist curl the natural lashes prior to applying the false lashes, when curling is necessary.

APPLICATION

False Lashes are generally applied after eye shadow and eyeliner have been applied.

STRIP LASHES

Hold the package in front of you, tips of lashes facing out, base of lashes facing you; the strip on the right side is for the right eye, and the strip on the left is for the left eye. Roll the strip off the bed with your thumbs, maintaining the shape of the lash. Fit the eyelash strip to your model's eye to determine if it needs trimming in the area where you will place it once the glue is affixed. If the lashes are too wide for your model's eye, trim the lashes, just a few hairs at a time, from the outside corner of the lashes. DO NOT do this while the lashes are on your model's eye. Do this before you glue the strip; after you have fitted them, try the fit again, after trimming, once more to gauge the placement of the strip.

With an orange-wood stick, apply the adhesive to the inside edge of the strip. Have your model look downward, holding the lashes with your fingertips in the center of the strip; tack the strip onto the area (it looks like a little ledge) directly above the model's natural lash line. (You need to keep it as close to the actual roots of the model's lashes as possible WITHOUT gluing it onto their actual lashes.) Continue to tack down the entire strip from the inside corner of the eyelid all the way to the outside corner. Check to ensure the strip is secure all the way across the lash line. Have your model continue to look down until the adhesive is dry, so that the strip doesn't move around once you have placed it. Once the strip lash is entirely dry you can put mascara on the lashes, adding more eyeliner on top of the lash line to blend it in if needed.

INDIVIDUALS

Remove these lashes from the eyelash bed. Dip the bead into the lash glue, and while your model is looking down, set the lash as close to the natural lash line as possible (lashes should be flaring up for upper lash line, and turned down for lower lash line). Space the lashes evenly across the eyelid, starting from the inside of the eye (using short lashes) and extending all the way across (using medium lashes) from "lash to lash." Have the tips of the lashes touch across the lash line; this will help to space the lashes evenly. For a more dramatic effect try stacking several rows of lashes on top of each other.

SINGLES

Are removed from the lash bed in the same manner as individuals, and applied with the same technique. These lashes work very well as lower lashes.

CHAPTER STUDY QUESTIONS

1. Is there only one method to curl lashes?

2. Does every make-up require that the artist curl the lashes.?

3. Can disposable mascara wands be reused?

4. Are fan brushes recommended only for cake mascara?

5. Is mascara applied only to the top lashes?

6. Does cream mascara builds and thickens lashes?

7. What should be used to sanitize eye lash curlers?

8. Do false lashes only come in one style?

9. Is it true that cake mascara generally colors, but does not thicken the lashes?

10. Cake mascara requires what other element to work?

CHAPTER 9
CHEEKS

The proper application technique for Cheek Color that appears natural and well blended will add life to the finished make-up. The make-up artist will be able to choose appropriate cheek colors for the model, as well as reinforce highlight and shadow on the cheekbone with Cheek Color products.

PHYSICAL FEATURES OF THE CHEEK

The cheekbone provides the lower portion of the frame for the eyes. Referring back to the eyebrow chapter, the eyebrows provided the upper frame for the eyes. Cheek color will add dimension to the cheekbones and ultimately create lift to the face as well as draw attention to the entire face.

Think of the cheekbone as a cylinder. It is the bone on the face that extends from approximately the middle of the ear to the corner of the eye. This bone is called the zygomatic arch. The depression under the cheekbone is where the cheekbone naturally curves inward, creating the base of the cylinder.

In this chapter, the areas of the cheekbone will be referred to as the following:

- The front of the cylinder is the area where the cheekbone begins on the face.
- The back is where the cylinder ends near the center of the ear.
- The top of the cylinder is where light hits the highest part of the cheekbone. This is where highlight is placed.
- The bottom of the cheekbone where the cheek curves inward. This is where shadow is placed.
- The center of the cheekbone is the area that is located between the top and the base of the cylinder. This is where cheek color is placed.

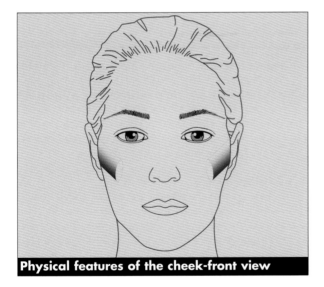
Physical features of the cheek-front view

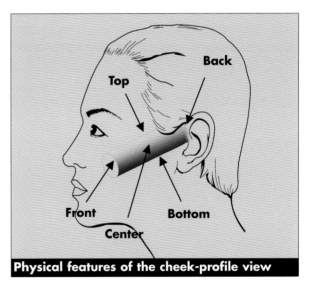
Physical features of the cheek-profile view

PLACEMENT OF CHEEK COLOR

After the make-up artist has completed the eye make-up treatments, the cheeks are next. The goal here is to create a natural and enhancing effect on the model. This is done with products known as cheek color or blush.

Cheek color is applied on the center of the cheekbone cylinder, along the length of the cheekbone. This is the mid-tone area of the cylinder. It begins at the hairline and stops at the corner of the eye, or where the cheekbone curves upward.

If the make-up artist chooses, highlights and shadows can be applied in the base application (refer to the Highlights and Shadows section of the cheekbone in the Corrective Make-Up chapter).

CHEEK COLOR PRODUCTS

Cheek colors are available in several product types, with powder and cream products being the most widely used. Becoming popular are cheek color gels, which are more translucent than powder or cream products, producing only a hint of color.

When using a powder cheek color, it is important that the model is adequately powdered. Powdering is the last step to the foundation application. If necessary, additional powder can be lightly applied prior to the application of cheek color.

Powder will slide over powder, ensuring a smooth and well blended application. If the model is not powdered properly the cheek color could adhere, leaving blotches of color on the cheeks.

When using a cream cheek color the artist will powder after the cheek color is applied. This becomes part of the building of the foundation process.

Cheek color gel is generally used when powdering is not necessary, keeping the application translucent.

POWDER CHEEK COLOR

To load the brush gently swipe a blush brush back and forth across the powder blush. Tap onto a clean tissue to remove any excess powder from the brush.

APPLICATION

• Begin at the back of the cheekbone near the hairline. Gently place the brush on the model's skin.

• Using a small circular motion, evenly move the brush from the back of the cheekbone to the front. If more color is desired, simply re-apply. It is easier to build up color from too light to more intense, than to lighten an application after too much product has been applied to the model's face.

Do not bring the powder cheek color too far forward on the cheekbone. Stop at the corner of the eye. Cheek color should not drop below the model's nostrils.

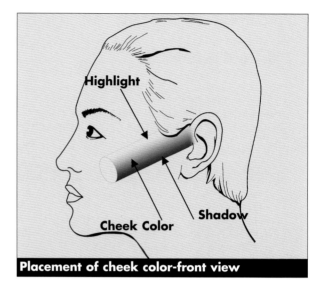

Placement of cheek color-front view

CREAM CHEEK COLOR

Many of the same principles of powder cheek color apply to cream cheek color. There are several important differences for the make-up artist to note.

Cream cheek color is wonderful for drier skins, or when a sheer wash of color is desired.

Due to the amount of slip, oilier skins should not use cream cheek colors. The same objectives and placement of powder cheek color apply to cream. The differences are in the sequence or application, and the tools used to apply cream cheek color.

Cream cheek color must be applied directly on top of base BEFORE POWDER. The reason is simple. Think cream to cream products. For a smooth, well-blended application, cream cheek color must go on top of an UNPOWDERED FOUNDATION APPLICATION. Cream adheres to cream. If the artist has already powdered the model's face, a cream cheek color will adhere and streak on the cheekbone. The combination will not result in smooth blending.

APPLICATION

The area of placement for cream cheek color is the same as powder cheek color: from the back of the cheekbone to the front, on the center of the cheekbone.

Cream cheek color may be applied with a sponge, a brush or the fingers.

After choosing the desired cheek color for the model, remove a small portion of the product with the palette knife. Place the product onto a clean make-up palette, using a clean make-up sponge/brush. Work some of the cream cheek color onto the sponge/brush. Smooth any lumps in the cream by tapping the sponge/brush back and forth on a clean area of the make-up palette. Begin placement of cheek color near the hairline (apply as if this were a base), working forward along the center of the cheekbone. Again, it is easier to build up color intensity with several light applications as opposed to putting too much product on and having to remove it if it is overdone. Be sure the edges of the cheek colo are

Applying powder cheek color

well blended so that there are no hard edges or streaks. When using your fingers to apply, begin with tapping the product on the center of the cheekbone, then gently blend with a light stroking motion.

GEL CHEEK COLOR

Gel cheek colors are generally transparent, creating a wash of color. This is especially nice when the make-up has that no make-up look and the cheeks require a hint of color.

When using gel as the cheek color, it is best not to have any powder in the make-up application. Powder will clump up when mixed with a gel. Cheek gels that are water-based dry quickly, and therefore are not recommended for dry skin. Other cheek gels that are not water-based dry less quickly and work well with drier skin.

To apply, refer to the application section of cream cheek color.

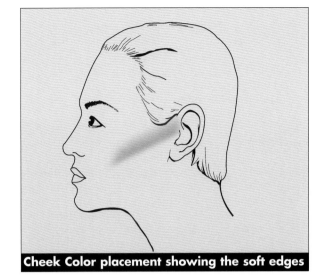
Cheek Color placement showing the soft edges

SELECTING COLOR

THE NATURAL LOOK

To choose cheek colors that look natural on the model's skin, follow these guidelines:

• The fairer the skin, the lighter the shades should be.

• Use colors such as light peach, apricot, soft pink and rose on light tones of skin.

• Medium tones may wear coral, soft beiges, warm rose and plums.

• Darker skin tones need more intense and deeper colors to be seen on the skin. Deep brick, rust, orange, dark plum and berry cheek colors work on darker skin tones.

HIGHLIGHT COLORS

When choosing the highlight color, make sure it is in the same family as the Cheek Color chosen Cheek Colors (the color chosen for the center of the cheekbone). However, the highlight color needs to be two to three shades lighter. Cheek Color as well as eye shadows may be used for this process. Extremely fair skins can be highlighted with pale shades of eye shadow, providing they are within the same tones as the Cheek Colors. An example of this would be: when soft apricot is the Cheek Color chosen for the center of the cheekbone the highlight colors could be pale peach or pale yellow, used along the top of the cheekbone to highlight the cheekbone.

SHADOW COLORS

To accent the base of the cheekbone, the shading color should be two to three shades deeper than the color chosen for the center of the cheekbone. Powder eye shadows may be used to accent the base of the cheekbone, if the cheek colors do not offer a variety of deep shades.

For darker skins, powder eye shadows such as a warm, deep brown can be used to shade the cheekbone if a brick or rust powder cheek color has been used on the center of the cheekbone.

Whatever the product or color chosen, it remains necessary to blend all areas of this application

COMMON COLOR MISTAKES

The following are some common mistakes that artists should avoid making in cheek color application.

Application Mistake:
Cheek color comes too far forward

Effect:
If the artist brings the cheek color too far forward on the model's face, it gives the effect of pulling the face down.

On a naturally thin face, a model may have very defined cheekbones (and consequently need no shading). Bringing the cheek color too far forward on this type of face will give the illusion of hollowing in the cheekbones even further, resulting in the model looking gaunt.

On a very full face that does not have defined cheekbones, bringing the cheek color too far forward pulls the focus of the face downward. This gives a model with a full face the illusion of jowls, which is not flattering and not the purpose of cheek color.

Application Mistake:
Too high on the cheekbone

Effect:
If the artist brings the cheek color too high (placed on the top of the cheekbone where highlight should be placed,) it has the effect of flattening the face. Instead of cheek color on the center of the cheekbone, giving the cheekbone dimension, the cheek color diminishes the balance the artist is trying to create on the model.

Application Mistake:
Too low on the cheekbone

Effect:
If the artist brings the cheek color too low on the cheekbone, by placing cheek color on the base/bottom of the cheekbone, it has the effect of lowering the model's natural cheekbone. This distorts the perception of natural cheekbone placement and diminishes the balance the artist is seeking to bring to the model's face.

Application Mistake:
Too much color on the cheekbone

Effect:
If the artist places too much cheek color on the cheekbone, it tends to overwhelm the face. The goal of a natural cheek color application is to bring warmth and a natural glow to the skin. Too much color often looks garish.

Application Mistake:
Too little color on the cheekbone

Effect:
Placing too little cheek color on the cheekbone defeats the purpose of applying cheek color.

Application Mistake:
Inadequately blended cheek color

Effect:
If the artist does not blend the edges of the cheek color on the cheekbone this will result in a stripe of cheek color instead of a soft, diffused blend along the cheekbone. For a smooth, even and natural looking application, remember to swirl the blush brush along the cheekbone in soft circles. This technique will help to ensure there are no harsh edges in the cheek color application.

CHAPTER STUDY QUESTIONS

1. What are the many terms for cheek color?

2. Which geometric shape does the cheekbone most resemble?

3. Cheek color is applied to what part of the cheek bone?

4. Are cheek colors only made from powder?

5. Are color gels more or less translucent?

6. What brush is used to apply powder cheek color?

7. What motion is suggested when applying powder cheek color?

8. Highlight is placed where on the cheekbone?

9. Shadow (contour) is placed where on the cheekbone?

10. Should cheek color have hard and soft edges?

CHAPTER 10

LIPS

The proper application of Lip Color will maintain balance and proportion to the lips. Lip color application is generally the last step in creating a beauty make-up. Done properly, it will pull the entire make-up together and give it life. After completing this chapter, the make-up artist will be able to apply lip color, outline to define the lips, and correct irregular lip shapes such as uneven lips, drooping lips, thin upper lip, thin lower lip, too-large lips, too-small lips, too-full lips, and lips that have no cupid's bow.

PHYSICAL FEATURES OF THE LIPS

The lips are a very soft and pliable tissue with a defined edge. This defined edge is known as the lip line and surrounds the upper and lower lip. The lip line indicates where the lip ends.

The upper lip usually has two peaks and a valley in the center. This is called a Cupid's Bow and can vary from person to person. Some Cupid's Bows will have more height, or perhaps more pointed peaks, while others may have a slightly more rounded edge to the peaks. Some upper lips may have no Cupid's Bow at all.

There is a natural highlight that surrounds the edge of the lips. This is called the labial roll. The labial roll adds to the dimension of the lip. On some people, the labial roll is very noticeable. Skin tone and width of the labial roll are factors that add to its appearance. Without this natural highlight around the lip, the lips tend to look flat, or lack dimension.

Throughout this chapter, reference will be made to the corners of the mouth. This is where the upper and lower lips meet.

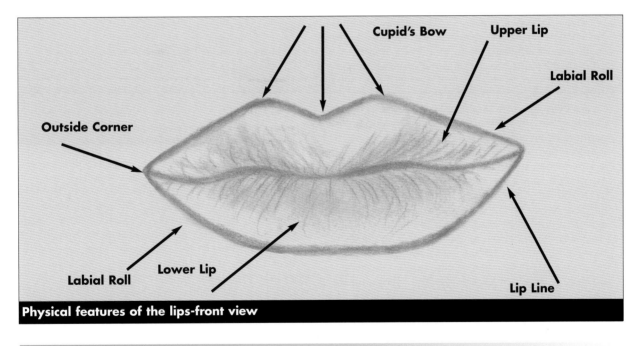

Physical features of the lips-front view

LIP COLOR APPLICATION

Before applying lip color the artist needs an understanding of the products used for this application. Several different products can be used, such as cream lip colors, matte lip color, or tinted lip gloss. These products come in several forms including lipsticks (lip color in a stick form) and lip color in pots such as lip gloss.

Cream lip color generally will contain some form of moisture, keeping the product moist whilst on the lips. This also aids in an easy smooth application. On lips that are rough or chapped the moisture content in a cream lip color will be more forgiving than other forms of lip color.

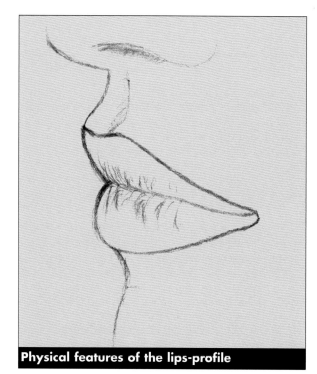

Physical features of the lips-profile

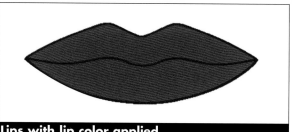

Lips with lip color applied

For basic lip color application, the make-up artist must first learn to load a lipstick brush. Getting the lip color from the tube and onto the brush can be done in several different ways.

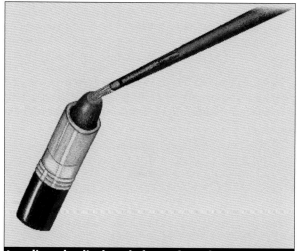

Loading the lip brush from the tube

Matte lip colors are generally dryer than cream and have little to no shine. Being dryer in nature they tend to have more staying power.

Lip color application is the procedure used to place a lip color product on the lips. Lip color will enhance the make-up application by drawing attention to the mouth. The lip color application is generally the last step in the make-up process, completing the make-up application for a total look.

Before applying lip color the condition of the lips needs to be evaluated, as lip care is an important factor when it comes to applying lip color. It is important to strive for a smooth application of lip color with defined edges at the lip line. The lips need to be smooth and in good condition. If the lips are rough or chapped, the lip color application will be rough and uneven. Therefore, just like exfoliating and then moisturizing the face, lips can also be exfoliated and moisturized if they are excessively dry. To maintain a healthy appearance the lips can be moisturized every day, with exfoliation as needed. Lip tissue is sensitive and care should be taken not to over-exfoliate. Use an exfoliating scrub and moisturizing cream to achieve smooth lips.

Lip color is applied to the upper and lower lip, staying within the lip line for a natural but well defined look.

The following illustration shows how the lips look when lip color has been applied.

One method is to take the lip brush directly to the tube and load from there; however, this method is recommended only if the tube is owned by the person it is used on (not used or shared with others.)

Another method is to use a palette knife to scrape a small amount from the tube, place it on a palette, then load the lip brush from there. An application using a brush is recommended to give a well defined, hard edge to the lip line.

To load the brush, work the color into the brush by dragging it through the lip color. A forward then backward motion, laying the brush almost flat through the product, works well to coat both sides of the brush. Be careful not to mash the brush tip into the product, as this will spread apart the bristles of the brush, resulting in an uneven application.

When the brush has been loaded with lip color, have the model open her mouth slightly and smile. This will tighten the lips so that they don't move during the application of lip color, allowing for a clean, crisp and sharp application of color.

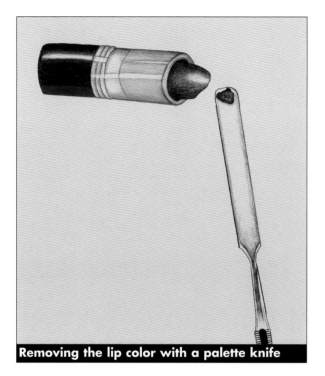

Removing the lip color with a palette knife

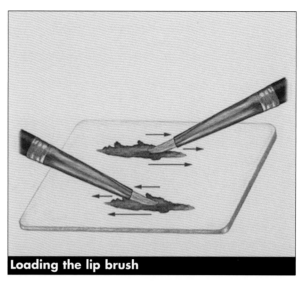

Loading the lip brush

UPPER LIP

• Place the brush on the outside corner of the mouth, laying the brush flat against the lip, with the outside edge of the brush against the edge of the lip.

• Drag the brush up towards the Cupid's Bow. When you reach the peak, turn the brush down, following the edge of the lip line to the center of the lip.

• Turn the brush over (this side should still be loaded with product) and repeat from the other side of the mouth.

• Reload brush.

LOWER LIP

• Placing the brush flat against the outside corner of the lip, follow the edge of the lip, dragging the brush towards the center. Once there, stop.

• Repeat the process from the other side of the mouth, stopping at the center.

• Have the model close her lips, and fill in the remaining area with product.

NOTE:

Keep the brush strokes flowing. After starting, don't break contact. Keeping a consistent amount of pressure on the brush will help to ensure an even application of product to the lips. Try to complete each lip with two strokes.

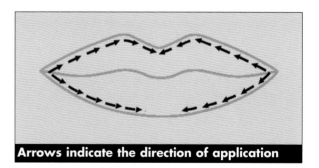

Arrows indicate the direction of application

LIP LINER APPLICATION

Lip liner application is a procedure used to apply lip pencil to the edge of the lip at the lip line. This method is done to create definition to the lips or to correct an irregularly shaped lip. By applying lip pencil to the lip line, it is possible to achieve a sharp, clean edge, by enhancing the appearance of the lips. It is not always necessary to line the lips, except when looking for that extra definition, or as outlined in the lip correction lesson that follows. These techniques for lip color application with the lip liner application will be combined for a completed look.

Once again, lip care is an important factor, as lips that are in good condition will have a smoother, more defined liner application, while lips that need to be exfoliated and/or moisturized are likely to have "skips or breaks" in the liner application.

Before each use, sharpen the lip pencil and spray with 99% alcohol. This will keep the pencil sharp and the application sanitary. It is not advised that a pencil be used on more than one person without first sharpening then sanitizing. A sharp pencil will help to achieve a fine, hard edge.

When using a lip pencil it is helpful to rest your pinky on the model's chin during the application procedure, to steady the hand.

UPPER LIP
• Have the model relax her mouth. Define the Cupid's Bow by starting at the center.

• Draw up to the peaks of the Cupid's Bow. From the peaks follow the lip line, being careful not to exceed the edge.

• Next, draw out to meet the outside corners of the mouth.

LOWER LIP
• Start at the outside corner and draw to the center of the lip.

• Repeat from the other side.

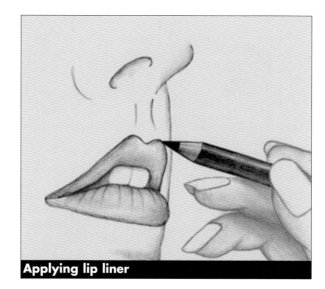
Applying lip liner

LIP LINER with LIP COLOR APPLICATION

Having practiced the elements of both the lip liner application and lip color application, they can be combined for a finished look.

Using a lip liner that is very close to the lip color will give a defined yet consistent look to the lips, while using a lip liner that is a shade darker than the lip color will give definition and depth to the lips. When using this technique it is important to pull the lip liner into the lip color by using a lip brush. This gives the illusion of depth to the lip line and creates a soft edge, keeping the look natural, not overdone.

Some cosmetic companies make a colorless or clear lip liner. This is used in the same manner as any other lip liner and is helpful when a soft or natural look is desired. This clear lip liner would be used with the addition of lip color and generally would not be used alone, keeping in mind it is colorless. This is a very effective process for a mature woman as it can be helpful in preventing bleeding of the lip color.

After the lip color has been applied, it is possible that there may be a need for more cheek color. Take an objective look when making that decision and remember to use the mirror as a guide.

When applying these techniques as the final portion of the beauty make-up application, the lips pull the finished make-up together, completing the look.

To keep organized and ultimately save time, be sure to have all the items out that are needed for the application. Sharpen and spray the lip pencil with 99% alcohol for a fine, sharp edge, and to keep the product sanitary.

• Line the natural lip line with the lip pencil as in the previous lesson. Be careful not to exceed the edge of the lip. Keep the pencil sharp, as a dull or rounded pencil cannot produce a fine line.

• Next, following the point-to-point method, fill in the lips with lip color.

• Use the different combinations of lip liner and lip color suggested earlier to see the varying effects that can be obtained.

While facing a mirror, look at the model. Seeing the model this way allows you to view your work from a different perspective.

LIP CORRECTION

Lip correction is the procedure used to identify and then correct irregular lip shapes. Keep in mind that the ultimate goal here is to create a balanced lip that not only is balanced to itself but is also balanced to the face. Since there are an endless variety of lip shapes, carefully study the differences. Some of those lip shapes may be a bit irregular, and others may be out of balance by a combination of irregularities. Either way,

some will need attention to help with correction while maintaining overall balance. The goal is to have as natural a lip as possible while correcting these irregularities. Often this requires only a slight adjustment, however, on occasions it may require a little more. Studying the variety of lip shapes in this lesson will give a better understanding of how to balance the lip.

Working with correcting irregular lip shapes may sometimes call for extending the lip line over the labial roll. The labial roll is the naturally highlighted portion of the lip that circles the mouth, giving it it's dimension. Because the lip has this highlight, care must be taken not to lose the highlight, or the lip will no longer have dimension, creating an unnatural or flat appearance. If this happens, the highlight must be replaced to maintain the naturalness of the lip. This can be done by using a light shade of base or using a highlight around the new lip line, blending to a soft edge.

Correcting lip shape is very important in balancing out the overall proportions of the face. Using a lip pencil will be helpful in achieving this.

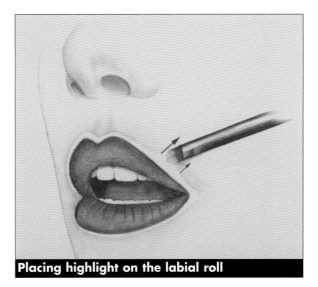

Placing highlight on the labial roll

LIP SHAPES

This illustration shows several of the many different lip shapes that the make-up artist will encounter. Some of these may be seen in combination. When correcting lip shape it is important to maintain balance.

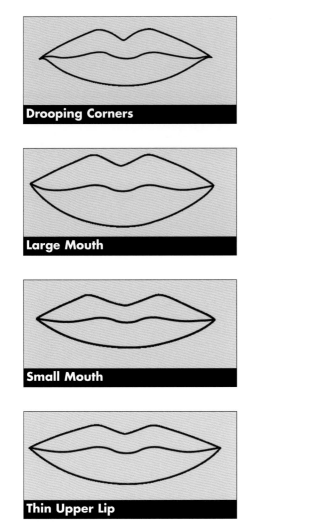

Drooping Corners

Large Mouth

Small Mouth

Thin Upper Lip

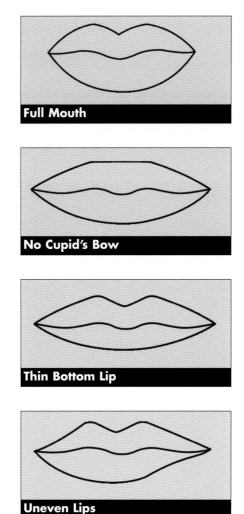

Full Mouth

No Cupid's Bow

Thin Bottom Lip

Uneven Lips

In this illustration the broken lines represent where to place lip liner to reshape/correct the lip shapes. Most often these adjustments are minor with effective results.

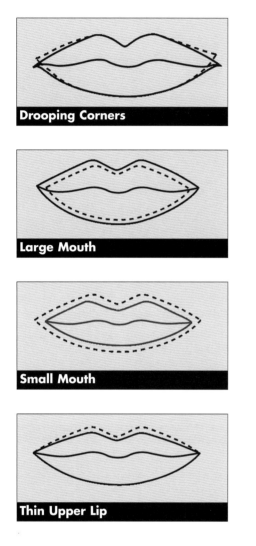

Drooping Corners

Large Mouth

Small Mouth

Thin Upper Lip

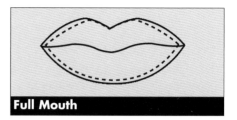

Full Mouth

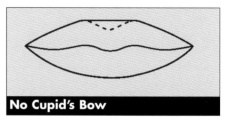

No Cupid's Bow

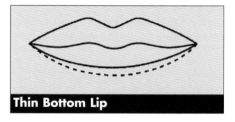

Thin Bottom Lip

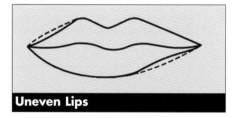

Uneven Lips

There are several observations that are required before correction of lip shapes can be approached. Standing in front of the model, look directly at her and ask yourself the following:

- Are the lips balanced to themselves?
- Is the upper lip larger than the lower lip?
- Is the lower lip larger than the upper lip?
- Is one side of the mouth drooping?
- Are the lips overall too thin?
- Are the lips out of proportion to the rest of the face?
- Is the upper lip (at the Cupid's Bow) defined?
- Do the corners of the mouth turn downward?

Within reason, corrections can be made for most of these situations.

Study the following examples. With a sharpened lip pencil, follow the examples. Draw in, or outline, to shape and balance the lips, then fill in with lip color, using the point-to-point method as previously described.

After applying, re-check by analyzing the shape of the lips. Look for balance and evenness from side to side and top to bottom.

After determining what type of lip shape, use a lip pencil to outline and adjust the shape of the lips as follows.

EXAMPLE:

• If the upper lip is slightly thinner than the lower lip, it is necessary to make the upper lip appear larger by drawing a line where the adjusted lip shape will be. Maintaining the naturalness of the lips is most important. Sometimes it will take only a slight adjustment to balance both the upper and lower lip.

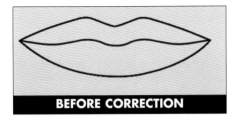

EXAMPLE:

• If the lower lip is quite a bit thinner than the upper lip, it is necessary to enlarge the lower lip by drawing and filling it in to balance the lip's top to bottom.

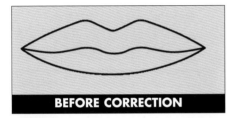

EXAMPLE:

• If one side of the lip is lower than the other, or uneven, it is necessary to draw and fill in the lower side to match the side that is not. Check the work to be sure that both sides have the same shape.

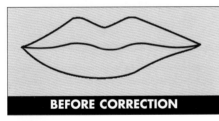

EXAMPLE:

• If the mouth appears small or out of balance with the rest of the face, it may be necessary to increase the size of both the upper and lower lip. Draw in the adjusted shape and fill in.

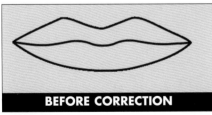

EXAMPLE:

• If the mouth appears large or out of balance with the rest of the face, it is necessary to decrease the size of both the upper and lower lip. Draw in the adjusted shape and fill in. The remaining exposed lip will be covered with base.

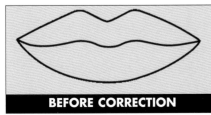

EXAMPLE:

• If the mouth has corners that droop, it is necessary to lift them by drawing across the lower lip in an upward motion and slightly filling in the upper lip at the corners, also in an upward motion.

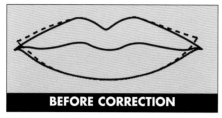

EXAMPLE:

• If the lips are full and out of balance with the rest of the face, it will be necessary to decrease the fullness of the lips by drawing inside the lip line on both the upper and lower lip. Once that is done, fill them in with lip color. The remaining exposed lip will be covered with base.

EXAMPLE:

• If the the upper lip is rounded and without a Cupid's Bow, it will be necessary create one by drawing it in and creating the peaks of the Cupid's Bow in the center of the upper lip. Follow by filling in with lip color.

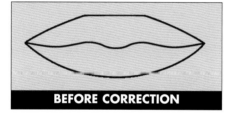

ON COLOR

• Light colors tend to make the lips appear larger, while dark colors may seem to diminish the size of a lip; this is based on the same theory as Highlights and Shadow. Highlights pull, shadows push.

• To blend a darker lip liner into a lighter lip color, apply lip pencil using a clean, dry lip brush to blend liner into the natural lip color. Apply light lip color to the center of mouth and blend to the lip line. This adds dimension and creates a soft transition of dark to light.

• To achieve a fuller look, apply a dab of a lighter shade of lip color, or a shimmery shade to the fullest part of the Cupid's Bow, and to the center of the bottom of the lip. For a variation of this, apply a lighter shade of lip color to the bottom lip only.

• When choosing a lip color the overall look to be achieved by the make-up artist will need to be taken into consideration. For example, for a natural make-up look, the color red would not be the right choice. However, a soft earthy pink would be a good selection.

• To achieve a classic period look of the fifties, soft peaches or pinks would not be the right choice. A bright classic red would be the color to choose. As with any make-up project, research will need to be done for accuracy.

CHAPTER STUDY QUESTIONS

1. Where is the Cupid's Bow located?

2. Lip liner is applied with what?

3. What is essential when applying lip color?

4. What is the natural highlight that surrounds the lip?

5. Dry lips may be helped by what?

6. Where do you start a lip liner application?

7. What is the purpose of applying lip liner?

8. When applying lip color, the brush is in what position?

9. Is lip color always matte in texture?

10. Should lip liner have a soft or a hard edge?

CHAPTER 11

PUTTING IT TOGETHER

Now it is time to combine the techniques and skills developed in the previous chapters for a complete make-up application, a total look. The make-up artist will develop a pattern of application to ensure consistent results, with confidence. The make-up artist will be able to create Natural, Fashion, Glamour and Trendy looks for both the youthful and mature face.

NATURAL/STRAIGHT MAKE-UP

Natural or Straight make-up does not necessarily mean that the model is not wearing any make-up. A natural make-up is a clean, soft make-up. The make-up artist will put together all or some of the following elements for a complete make-up in this order: base/foundation, powder, eyebrows, eye shadow, eyeliner, mascara, cheek color, lip color. Select neutral and warm color choices for eyes, cheeks and lips. Use colors that harmonize with the model's skin tone, eyes and hair color. Think in terms of warm browns, beiges and creams, soft peaches and light neutral browns. This is not the look for a glamour eye shadow treatment or a heavy eyeliner application. Think in terms of clean or fresh beauty. The look should enhance the appearance of the skin, eyes and lips without making the model appear as if she is wearing excess make-up.

APPLICATION

It is suggested that make-up be applied in the following order.

• Assess the model's face and skin type.

• Cleanse, tone and moisturize the model's face with appropriate skin-care products as needed.

• Assess the model's eyebrows. If necessary, brush, trim or tweeze to shape the eyebrows.

• Choose an appropriate base for the model's skin type and coverage that is desired. Apply the chosen base. Use a concealer for any skin discolorations, if needed. Be sure that the base is well blended (typically for a natural look, base coverage is sheer to medium).

• Depending on product choices (powder or cream),

this may be the time to powder the model's skin to set the base.

• Apply appropriate eyebrow color to the eyebrows, balancing and defining the brows.

• Choose warm tones to highlight and shadow the eyes, incorporating the techniques used for shadow placement based upon eye folds. Use small amounts of product on the eye color brush, keeping shadows soft and well blended. The artist will choose whether to place a drop shadow or not on the model.

• Apply eye liner, using cake, pencil or powder. Keep the application light and well blended. Apply straight or natural eyeliner with softened edges (as opposed to hard edges, which are more dramatic). Keep the shades of eyeliner neutral, using black or brown.

• Curl lashes and apply mascara. Choose either brown or black mascara.

• Apply cheek color. Choose warm neutral tones. Keep the edges very well blended so there are no hard edges on the top or bottom of the cheekbone.

• If needed, apply lip liner bringing the upper and lower lip into balance. Use neutral tones close to the lips' natural color.

• Apply lip color. Choose colors that are in the same tones as the cheek color choices. Keep colors neutral and soft.

When applying make-up, keep in mind the theory of less is more. In other words, use only what you need and do not apply make-up just for the sake of applying it.

FASHION AND GLAMOUR MAKE-UP

It is generally accepted that Fashion and Glamour make-up applications are more dramatic in their look. The make-up applications are usually for darker lighting situations, or when creating a particular character look. Fashion and Glamour make-up applications may allow for the use of stronger highlights and shading, and iridescent and vibrant color choices, as opposed to the muted, neutral color choices for a natural make-up. However, this does not mean that neutral tones cannot be used. Black may beconsidered a neutral tone, yet when it is applied properly it will give a beautiful dramatic look to the eyes.

APPLICATION

It is suggested that make-up be applied in the following order.

• Assess the model's face and skin type.

• Cleanse, tone and moisturize with the appropriate skin-care products as needed.

• Assess the model's eyebrows. Brush, trim or tweeze as needed to shape.

• Choose an appropriate base for the model's skin type and coverage that is desired. Apply the chosen base. Use a concealer for any skin discolorations, if needed. Be sure that the base is well blended. The base does not change in amount of coverage. Changes will be seen primarily in the eye treatment with subtle changes to cheeks and lips.

• Highlight and shadow (contour) any areas needed, such as the nose, cheekbones or jaw-line.

• Depending on product choices (powder or cream), this may be the time to powder the model's skin to set the base.

• Apply appropriate eyebrow color to the eyebrows, balancing and defining the brows.

• Using the techniques the make-up artist has learned for Fashion and Glamour eye treatments, choose highlight and shadow colors. More layers of shadow may be used to achieve a dramatic effect. Iridescent colors and shadows, as dark as black, can be incorporated in a fashion or glamour eye shadow treatment.

• Eye liner may be applied with any combination of eye shadow, cake eye liner, and pencil to draw attention to the eyes and enhance the eye shadow treatments. The make-up artist will choose a natural, fashion, or glamour eye liner. Hard edges may be used in the eye liner treatments for this look.

• Curl lashes and apply black mascara for a dramatic look, to the upper and lower eye lashes. A second coat may be applied to thicken and lengthen lashes even more. False lashes may be considered, as an option, to enhance the drama of the eyes.

• If powder is your choice for cheek color now would be the time to apply. Cheek color in a deeper shade than what would be used in a natural make-up may be an option.

• Apply lip liner, bringing balance to, or correcting the upper and lower lips.

• Apply lip color. For a Fashion or Glamour look, the make-up artist can choose from a wide array of colors and textures; light and dark colors, iridescent, matte, or glossy finishes.

When doing any make-up application, it is important to establish an order to follow. This will keep the application organized and will, with practice, build speed and confidence.

TRENDS AND CHANGE

Trendy means the latest trend or style. Style is in constant flux in fashion and make-up; which simply means this year's hot new look will be next year's tired old style.

Make-up, like clothing trends, changes every year. Cosmetic companies continuously come out with new colors and textures. This helps to stimulate the market, and gives the make-up artist "new products" to play with.

Trendy make-up is playful and fun. It uses a wide array of colors, shimmer and shine. The make-up artist is unlimited in the array of looks and color combinations available to apply.

Trendy make-ups incorporate all the techniques the artist has learned and practiced. The basic rules apply, no matter what look is to be achieved:

• Base should be applied consistently with appropriate color choice.

• Highlights pull. Shadows push.

• Matte colors tend to absorb light.

• Iridescent colors reflect light.

• Build eye shadow treatments in small increments.

• Balance overall.

• And remember to blend, blend, blend!

APPLICATION

The following is a suggested application. This will change according to the desired look to be achieved. Not all trendy make-up applications will have every step, as not all looks require the use of, for example, an eye liner application. Each make-up should be customized to the face and the look desired.

• Assess the model's face and skin type.

• Cleanse, tone, and moisturize the model's skin with the appropriate skin care products as needed.

• Assess the model's eyebrows. If necessary, brush, trim or tweeze to shape the eyebrows.

• Choose the appropriate base for the model's skin type and coverage that is desired. Apply the chosen base. Use a concealer for any skin discolorations, if needed. Be sure base is well blended and that the coverage is sheer to medium, depending on how this make-up will be viewed or shot.

• Powder the model's skin to set the applied base.

• Choose two to five eye shadow colors to apply to the model. Decide what type of eye shadow treatment to apply to the model; choices may be soft to intense, clean to smokey, or matte to an iridescent luster.

• Choose an eye liner product and apply an eye liner position that enhances the overall look of the make-up. Example: For a smokey eye, one choice may be to use a fashion eyeliner treatment with a smudged drop shadow reinforced with eye liner, in black, around the eye.

• Curl the lashes and apply mascara. The artist may definitely choose different color mascaras, or perhaps consider it more appropriate to use false lashes.

• Apply cheek color, either powder, cream or gel cheek color.

• Use a lip liner, if needed, to bring the upper and lower lip into balance.

• Apply lip color. For a high-impact mouth, apply lip gloss on top of lip color.

• When the make-up is complete, view the application in a mirror; this will give a truer reading of how the camera will see the application.

THE MATURE FACE

It is important to pay specific attention to the needs of the mature face when creating a total look.

The mature face should not be heavy or it may tend to look over-done. Remember, less is more in this make-up design. The make-up should be flattering, with only neutral and natural colors being used from the make-up artist's palette.

Avoid using bright colors, as they will look harsh on mature women. All lines should be soft in this application, with no hard edges. The final effect of this make-up should be an overall enhancement to the mature face, smoothing the skin and bringing gentle color and definition to the face.

APPLICATION

It is suggested that make-up be applied in the following order.

• Assess the model's face and skin type.

• Cleanse, tone, and moisturize the model's skin with the appropriate skin care products.

• Assess the model's eyebrows. If necessary, brush, trim or tweeze to shape the eyebrows.

• Choose the appropriate base for the model's skin type and coverage that is desired. Apply the chosen base. Use a concealer for any skin discolorations, if needed. Be sure base is well blended.

• Lightly powder the model's skin to, set the base, if necessary. The mature face requires very little, if any, powder. Powder on the mature face can have an adverse effect, aging instead of flattering.

• Apply highlight and shadow to areas that might need contouring. Remember that most mature women will need more highlights than shadows.

• Cream cheek color can be applied at this point. Choose a warm color that looks natural on the model. Employ the techniques learned in the cheek color chapter for cream cheek color application.

• If necessary, lightly dust loose powder to set the make-up. Do not over powder any areas, as powder might settle into creases.

• Color, shape, and softly define the eyebrows, using pencil or powder in neutral shades of taupe to warm brown.

• Apply the appropriate eye color treatment to the eyes, paying special attention to eyes with a heavy fold and recessed eyes. Use soft, neutral/natural tones to shade and highlight the eyes, such as creams, warm light apricot, and soft medium browns, in matte finishes. Avoid iridescent colors, as they reflect light and draw attention to any part of the skin that is crepy or wrinkled.

• Use neutral eye shadows (dry or wet) or cake eye liner, and smudge to soften the effect. Pay attention to the model's eye fold and be sure the liner doesn't accentuate any heavy folds or drooping of the eyelid. Keep the drop shadow simple, not wide or heavy. Do not close in the corners of the eye in this make-up.

• Apply one light coat of mascara in natural tones to upper and lower lashes. Avoid smudges, clumps or globs of mascara on the lashes. If desired, comb through the lashes with a lash brush to remove any excess or unwanted mascara.

• When applying lip liner pencil to the mature face, be attentive to the corners of the mouth. Use the corrective techniques for drooping corners, and thin lips when called for.

• Choose lip liner color in warm tones such as rose, light berry, coral, and apricot; a lip liner pencil helps act as a barrier to minimize bleeding of lip colors.

• Choose a shade of lip color. Select lip colors in lighter, warm shades in the same color families to complement cheek color and lip liner pencil colors used for the model. Harmonizing the cheek and lip colors will complement the skin and will look simple and elegant. Use a lip brush to fill in the lip color. Contain lip color within the bordered lines of the lip pencil. Gloss, dark colors, and matte finishes are not recommended for the mature model.

• Powder the lips of the mature model at this time to allow for the lip color to "hold" onto the lips firmly, and, again, to minimize bleeding of lip colors.

• After the make-up is complete, look at the model's face in the mirror. Check for any final adjustments that may be deemed necessary.

CHAPTER STUDY QUESTIONS

1. A natural make-up application should be what?

2. Should eye liner be used in every make-up?

3. What are trends?

4. Can a glamour eye make-up treatment be used in a natural looking make-up?

5. Are neutral colors best used for a natural make-up?

6. What eye treatments are used for a dramatic look?

7. Vibrant colors are used for what type of look?

8. Is it true that when dealing with trendy make-up, it is not necessary to be concerned with highlight and shadow?

9. Why is it important to have an order in which to apply make-up?

10. Should natural make-up have mostly soft edges?

CHAPTER 12
MATURE MAKE-UP

Make-up for the mature woman takes finesse and delicate balance. In this chapter the make-up artist will develop the proper make-up application and techniques required to meet the needs of a mature facial structure.

FEATURES OF THE MATURE FACE

As women get older their facial structure changes significantly. The key cause for this change is gravity, and with gravity comes a pull-down effect. Everything on the face is affected by the aging process, with certain areas of the face being more affected than others.

The folds of the eyes, under the eyes, the nasolabial folds, the jowls, the corners of the mouth, and the skin of the neck are the most common areas to be affected by this downward slide; this creates shadows in unflattering places.

Another factor is the condition of the mature skin. As the aging process takes over, the moisture in the skin depletes. When the skin loses moisture, it also loses elasticity. Lines or wrinkles develop, leaving the skin in a dry state. Some of the aging effects of the face can be improved upon by a daily regimen of skin-care maintenance. With mature skin it is very important to replenish lost moisture. This aids in keeping the skin supple. Discoloration of the skin, such as age spots, can also be seen in the mature face. Ultimately, a good skin regimen enhances the make-up application.

These are the combined elements that the artist must address when applying make-up to the mature woman.

ANALYZING THE MATURE FACE

The overall make-up concept for the mature woman is to improve upon the existing features of the Mature face. It is not necessarily to create a youthful appearance, but a skillful make-up application sometimes may result in one.

A great make-up artist develops a critical eye. The artist sees details and analyzes the face to know the positive and negative aspects of the model's face.

The positive aspects are enhanced as the negative aspects are diminished. This gives balance to the face while improving the overall look of the individual.

Positive aspects may be bright colorful eyes, excellent skin tone, long lashes or well-defined eyebrows.

Negative aspects may be thinning eyebrows, heavy folds on the eyes, puffiness or bags under the eyes, deep set lines at the nasolabial folds or across the forehead, age spots or discoloration to the skin tone, dark circles under the eyes and deep set lines around the lips. The latter is particularly the case when the person is a smoker.

With the mature make-up application it is a matter of seeing then correcting the negative aspects of the face.

After the make-up artist recognizes this in the face, the artist customizes the most effective make-up application for the model. This will vary from individual to individual.

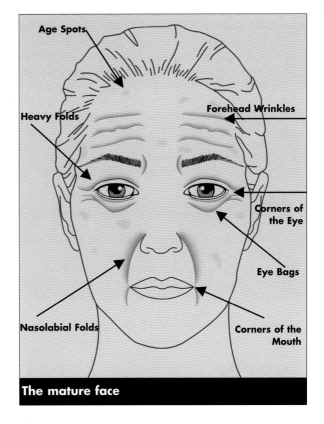

The mature face

(Labels: Age Spots, Heavy Folds, Nasolabial Folds, Forehead Wrinkles, Corners of the Eye, Eye Bags, Corners of the Mouth)

BUILDING THE FOUNDATION

A light application of moisturizer before applying base will help to improve any dry area of the skin. Dry skin may prevent a smooth application of base and may cause the base to streak. Too much moisturizer on the skin may cause the base to slide on the surface, moving away from where it was originally placed.

As in most make-up applications, make-up is applied only where it is needed, using the least amount possible. This most certainly applies when working on mature women. Because wrinkles generally exist, a heavy application of base will only make them more noticeable.

STEP 1–BASE

Analyze the face/skin. Apply moisturizer if needed. Choose a base color to match. With a mature woman, there may be several colors in the skin tone. Locate a medium shade on the face between the lighter shades and the darker shades seen. The base may need to be mixed to obtain the correct match. Undertone is important. Generally a mature person will need some olive in the base, as certain women tend to get an ash tone with age. When this is the case, the ash tone can make a person seem cold or unhealthy looking. Olive in the base will help to create a warming tone to the skin.

Put a small amount of base on the palette. From the palette, load the base on the make-up sponge. Check the sponge to ensure an even coverage of base. This will minimize possible streaking during application.

Begin the base application at the hairline on the forehead. Work the base down to the eyebrows. Re-load the sponge as needed. Continue to cover the remainder of the face and neck, leaving the eye area to be applied last, blending off the neck to prevent a noticeable change in color where the make-up stops.

When complete, check the application. Look for any areas that may need extra coverage, such as age spots that still show through the base. Other areas to be aware of are under the eyes and the inside corners of the eyes.

STEP 2–CAMOUFLAGE

Use the same techniques to conceal irregular skin-tones from the Base chapter. Choose a color that is close to the model's skin tone. When working with mature skin it may help to mix the concealer with a small amount of base. This creates a base-tone relationship and gives more slip to the concealer. Use the palette when mixing.

A concealer or small eye shadow brush works well to apply concealer to the hard-to-reach areas such as the corners of the eyes. This gives the artist more control over the placement of the product.

Once the areas that require concealer are covered use the sponge with base, tapping lightly, blending the areas together.

STEP 3–HIGHLIGHT AND SHADOW

At this point the face should be even in color and coverage. Using either a lighter foundation or lighter concealer mixed with foundation, highlight the corners of eyes, any deep set lines on the forehead, the nasolabial folds, top of the cheek bone, the temples and the corners of the mouth. Once again, just a light touch with a small amount of make-up should be adequate. Tap these areas with the base sponge to blend.

Usually mature women will need more highlights than shadows. An area that might need shadow will be the jaw line. Mix the shadow color with base to ensure the base-tone relationship.

Mature skin seems to do better with little to no powder. Powder can settle into the lines of the face when too much of it is used, making the lines of the face more noticeable. Remember, less is more!

EYES

Now that the foundation is complete, the artist has a fresh, even canvas for application of the remaining make-up elements. Keeping within the neutral tones for a natural looking make-up is the best way to approach a mature make-up. Bright colors such as blues and greens do not work well with mature women. Mature faces need softness in all aspects of make-up, especially with color and blending.

EYEBROWS

The shape of the eyebrows should be natural without any harsh edges or abrupt arches. Tweezing underneath will ensure lift and open up the eye.

EYE SHADOW

With the eyes framed from the eyebrows, the next step is to apply eye shadow. Analyze what type of an eye fold the person has. It probably will have drooped with age and therefore most likely should be treated similarly to the heavy fold or, in some cases, as a recessed eye. The skin in this part of the eye may be wrinkled or crepy. It is recommended that you stay away from any shadow colors that are iridescent. Iridescent colors will show the inconsistencies in the wrinkled skin, making them more noticeable. As with most make-up applications, the artist creates illusions; this is most definitely so with a mature make-up.

EYE LINER

Applying eye liner to a mature eye takes skill, but a few simple techniques can result in   success. The biggest factor is the possible lack of smooth skin; eye shadow will help smooth the skin and, therefore, assists in an easier eye liner application.

LASHES & MASCARA

A thin layer of mascara is generally adequate to finish the eye make-up treatment.

EYE APPLICATION

EYEBROWS

Brush the eyebrows in an upward direction before adding product. Trim and/or tweeze to shape. Colors should begin light, building by adding a shade or two darker to keep dimension. Using an eyebrow pencil, combined with eye shadow, will maintain the softness of a natural eyebrow. Remember that eyebrows are rarely exact, particulary where a mature woman is concerned.

EYE SHADOW

Remember, highlights pull and shadows push. With this in mind look for any areas that need to be pulled forward. This is where highlight will be placed. Look for the heaviest part of the fold. This is where shadow will be placed. Use soft creams or yellow for highlight and taupes or medium warm browns for shadow. Stay with warm tones, avoiding bright blues, bright greens and black, for the mature make-up application. These colors are harsh and will make a mature woman appear hard. Blending all of the edges in this eye shadow application is a must. Shadow colors have to blend together to keep the make-up soft and natural.

EYE LINER

To avoid hard, messy or skipped liner, it is best to stay away from liquid liners. Cake liner that has been smudged or an application using eye shadows work best for the mature eye. Soft edges can be obtained with either application. Color choices are generally limited to medium browns, dark browns, charcoal or black.

When using eye shadow, tap a small angle or wedge brush into the eye shadow. Tap both sides of the brush for an even amount of product. Following the guidelines for eye liner application, gently tap the product across the upper lid at the lash line, following the contour of the eye.

When using a cake liner, use an eye liner brush. Work the dampened brush into the product in a circular motion, making a slurry. Following the guidelines for eye liner application, apply the eye liner. Next, soften the edges of the eye liner with a slightly wet angle or wedge brush to create a soft edge. When dampening the brush, be sure not to have too much moisture on it; this will lift the product back onto the brush and off of the eye lid. Too little moisture on the brush will cause the product to flake.

LASHES & MASCARA

Curl the lashes, if needed. For mature women, dark brown or black mascara would be the color of choice. Do not choose brightly colored mascara. Apply, following the guidelines previously established. Keep the application light and be sure to apply not only to the Upper Lashes but the Lower Lashes as well. When using cream mascara watch for clumping, keeping the application consistent.

CHEEKS

As with most Mature Women the make-up application needs to have an uplifting effect. Placement of the cheek color becomes most important in the mature make-up application. Cheek color applied correctly can add to the illusion of lift. Applied incorrectly, it can add to the drag or downward motion of the face.

Maintain the idea of a natural-looking make-up; using less is more concept. This is important because the mature woman may have drier skin. Excess make-up can create an aging effect, instead of portraying a more youthful appearance. The softness of the chosen shade with blended edges will enhance the overall make-up.

CHEEKS APPLICATION

Keep the application of cheek color/blush light. Once again, with skin that may not be as smooth as it once was, too much make-up will have the opposite effect of what you are trying to achieve.

Soft colors such as a pale rose or light apricot give a glow to the cheek. Dark colors will have a contouring effect on a mature woman. With a cheek color or blush brush apply a very light coating to the cheek. Begin at the hairline and in a small circular motion work toward the front of the cheekbone. Follow the guidelines for applying cheek color, being careful not to bring the cheek color too far forward.

Warm colors will give life to the make-up application, whereas cool colors on mature skin will age that person.

LIPS

The lips need particular attention. The corners of the mouth are likely to show signs of drooping. There may be lines around the mouth ranging from slight to quite deep. This may be the case, especially if this person is a smoker. This means that when lip color is applied it could find it's way into those lines. This is called bleeding. Dark lip colors will show bleeding more than lighter lip colors.

The Lips are the final step in a mature make-up application. After completion, observe and analyze the entire make-up, making any final adjustments.

LIP COLOR APPLICATION

If the lines surrounding the lips are noticeable, base and powder applied over the lips can help to minimize bleeding. Another method that works well here is to apply a lip pencil to the lip line. This acts as a dam, aiding in stopping the lip color from bleeding.

Use a lip pencil that is the same shade as the lip color to be used. Using the corrective methods discussed in the lip chapter, line the lips. Remember to keep the pencil sharp. Choose a lip color that is a matte finish, not a gloss. Apply lip color, up to the lip line. A soft natural rose or peach color is a good choice. Stay within the lip line, not over it. By keeping the Lip Color inside the lip line a barrier is created.

Another useful method involves a colorless powder, a tissue and a brush.

Separate a tissue. Tissue is generally two-ply; however, for this you need only one-ply. Place the tissue onto the lips. With a cheek color or blush brush apply powder directly over the tissue using a light tapping motion. This will place a light dusting of powder onto the lip color. With a clean brush, dust off excess loose powder. Reapply lip color.

This step may be repeated for long wear.

CHAPTER STUDY QUESTIONS

1. How much powder should be used on a mature make-up ?

2. What type of colors are a good choice for this type of make-up?

3. Lip color is likely to bleed with a mature face?

4. Do dark or bright colors work with this make-up?

5. Why is skin care important?

6. What type of folds may be found in the mature face?

7. How are age spots dealt with?

8. Should the nasolabial fold be corrected?

9. Why is an uplifting effect important in this make-up?

10. What type of eye liner treatment is recommended?

CHAPTER 13

BRIDAL MAKE-UP ———————————————

Bridal make-up is perhaps one of the most controversial make-ups today. What exactly is a bridal make-up? Simply put, it is whatever the bride wants it to be. A wedding may be considered a society make-up or a photo shoot. Numerous weddings are now video taped and even more weddings are using both mediums to capture the day. Today there are more themed weddings than ever before, so a bridal make-up may even be considered a character make-up. The make-up is individualized and of course will need to be adjusted for each and every bride.

THE PROCESS

CONSULTATION

There are many things to consider in doing bridal make-up, and for this reason, communication with the bride is of the utmost importance. A consultation with the bride is recommended to find out what type of make-up she has in mind.

Use the consultation to get as much information about the wedding as you can, such as:

- The time of day; morning, afternoon or evening

- The season; spring, summer, fall or winter

- The location (city/state) of the wedding

- Indoors (place of worship), outdoors (park, ocean)

- Discuss the use of colors in the wedding (flowers, bridesmaid dresses, etc.).

- How are they planning on wearing their hair?

- What are they wearing in or on their hair, flowers, hat or veil?

- What style of dress; formal, casual, sexy, period?

- The color of her dress; white, off-white, warm or cool?

- How many people will need make-up? – does the groom need or want make-up?

The consultation should include and consider all the details of the style of wedding, so that the make-up is in harmony, not at odds, with the overall look of the wedding: A typical American bride would have soft natural make-up, using soft cool colors or soft warm colors, whatever looks best with her coloring, and possibly her dress. If the bride comes from a different culture, find out what would change. For instance, a Persian bride usually likes more exotic eyes and darker lips. During your consultation you will find out exactly what the bride wants.

DO A TEST MAKE-UP

A test make-up is recommended, to establish a relationship with the bride and to design the make-up, prior to the day of the wedding. Once the make-up artist and bride are happy with the test it is wise to record the work. Take a photo of the make-up, preferably with a Polaroid camera. Take continuity notes, for future reference.

The make-up test is a good time to discuss fees; there are no set rules- the artist can charge by the person, the hour, or the day, whichever you prefer.

It is a good idea to collect a portion of your fee (up to 50%) at the make-up test. Be sure to include such items as excessive travel or mileage, parking fees, etc. It is recommended that you collect your fees before the wedding, since there is usually a lot of excitement and confusion during the wedding, and you may have to remind them to pay you, if you can find them, that is.

THE MAKE-UP

If the wedding is in the spring the make-up will more than likely be soft natural shades with glowing soft cheeks. This creates a healthy look, reminiscent of springtime. If the wedding is in the evening, and more formal, the make-up can be additionally dramatic, smoky eyes, or darker or red lips, rather than the clean natural daytime look with soft pinks or peaches. A period wedding requires the make-up of that time, a 1940s wedding, with soft natural eyes, thin long false lashes and red lips. Keep in mind that different cultures may impact the make-up style. Whatever the choice, consider using water resistant products, such as foundations, lip stains, lip ink, waterproof mascara and possibly waterproof eyeliner as a safeguard, since crying is not unusual at a wedding.

If the make-up artist is not staying through for the touch-ups, leave a touch-up kit for the bride that includes powder, lipstick and lip liner. You might want to have her purchase them beforehand.

MARKETING YOURSELF

Weddings can be a lucrative source of income for the free-lance make-up artist. Consider having a detailed contract. The contract should include the wedding date, the wedding address, the bride's address (or responsible billing party), mileage, the number of people needing make-up (including children and men), fees for yourself as well as fees for assistants needed, and all other details pertaining to the wedding day. Also, include the date of the test make-up application and possibly a deposit to book the date. You may even want to consider a cancellation clause. Advertise at bridal shops, newspapers, magazines, etc. It's good to establish a relationship with a local bridal shop or consultant, do demonstrations from time to time to help drum up interest, and/or create a separate Bridal Portfolio. Make sure you stay in touch with the photographers you meet at weddings, so you can get photos for your portfolio. Have your business cards with you at all times to hand out.

CHAPTER STUDY QUESTIONS

1. Is it important to have a consultation with the bride?

2. What type of make-up application would you use for a wedding?

3. Why is it important to consider the time of day of the wedding?

4. Why is it important to consider the time of year of the wedding?

5. How is the make-up different for a casual versus a formal wedding?

6. Why do a test make-up?

7. Should you take business cards to a wedding?

8. Should you have a contract?

9. Would a separate Bridal Portfolio be beneficial?

10. Should you charge for additional people?

CHAPTER 14

FACE-LIFTS AND MALE CORRECTIVE

Face-lifts, as they relate to the mature face, can reduce signs of aging in both women and men. This is done by lifting and re-positioning the facial tissue, giving the illusion of tighter, younger skin. Face-lifts may also be used to aid in the creation of a character, such as creating an Asian looking eye on a Caucasian.

PHYSICAL FEATURES OF FACE-LIFTS

The face-lift is composed of three parts; the leading edge, the link, and the fastener.

The leading edge is the portion of the lift that attaches to the skin. This may be made of a tape or lace type material. The link is the portion of the lift that is attached to the leading edge. The link is usually made of an elastic material, such as a rubber band. The fastener is the portion of the lift that secures the two sides together. The fastener may be made of many different materials, such as paper clips, wire, string, and plastic tabs that lock.

In a very raw and simple form, the face-lift may be duct tape, attached to either side of the neck, thus pulling the loose skin tight.

The make-up artist may purchase face-lifts over the counter or, when the need arises, custom make them to suit his/her needs.

OVER THE COUNTER FACE LIFTS

Over the counter face-lifts are conveniently ready to apply right out of the box, as they are adjustable to fit any size face. Some disadvantages, however, to an over counter face–lift are that they may be somewhat expensive, or that the tape doesn't always take well to make-up, making it difficult to conceal especially if the model has short hair.

CUSTOM MADE FACE LIFTS

There may be an occasion when custom face lifts are required, or you may want to avoid the cost of over the counter face-lifts; in that event use wig lace for the leading edge, and adhesive to secure the lace to the skin. Rubber bands can be used for the links with paper clips as the fasteners. Although not very high tech this type of face-lift is very easy and inexpensive to make. One advantage to using wig lace for the leading edge is its ability to be hidden against the skin fairly easily.

FACE-LIFTS APPLICATION

Analyze the model's face, with the model facing the mirror, observing where the loose skin needs tightening. Most often the areas of concern will be the neck and jaw area, as well as the skin across the cheeks, which affects the nasolabial fold. The temple area can help the skin around the eyes.

Use your fingers to gently pull up in the areas you feel need lift. Re-position your fingers as needed. This will serve as a guideline for placing the face-lifts. While doing this, keep in mind that the idea is to enhance the features. If the skin is pulled excessively tight the skin will become distorted and the face will no longer appear natural.

LEADING EDGE APPLICATION

Once you have determined the position of the leading edge for the face-lifts, use a cotton swab with 99% alcohol to clean the area where the leading edge will be secured. If using over the counter face-lifts, simply remove the protective coating from the tape. If you are using wig lace you will need to apply a small amount of a medical adhesive to the skin at this time. Position the leading edge and gently apply pressure to secure it in place. Pull the link across the back of the head and secure the fastener in place.

It may be necessary to use more than one set of face-lifts. If this is the case the lifts may be secured by criss-crossing them across the back of the head.

Once the face-lifts are in place it is necessary to conceal them. Use the model's hair, providing the model has enough length to their hair to do this, in order to cover all exposed parts of the face-lift. The hair should be pulled forward to cover each piece of the face-lift. When the hair is too short a wig, hat or scarf may be used to conceal the face-lifts.

To remove the face-lifts start by unhooking the fasteners. Next, use a 99% alcohol soaked cotton swab to work the area of the leading edge until it becomes loose. Gently lift the loosened edge, while continuing to apply the alcohol, until the leading edge lifts off the skin completely. Once the face-lifts are off, clean the skin thoroughly.

When using wig lace as the leading edge, it is important to clean the lace thoroughly with 99% alcohol before re-using; otherwise the medical adhesive may leave a white residue on the lace.

MALE CORRECTIVE

The concept of a male corrective make-up is to enhance the positive features, playing down the negative features without removing his character. This make-up is generally a light application, so as not to take away the fact that he is male. Heavy make-up on a man may feminize him; you should only apply make-up where needed.

APPLICATION

• Using an anti-shine product before applying any make-up will help ensure a matte finish, requiring less powdering after the make-up is complete.

• Base match with as minimal coverage as possible. Mixing the base with a cream moisturizer will ensure sheer application.

• Utilize the corrective palette if needed.

• A hint of cheek color.

• When the model is fair-haired, light brow gel or cake mascara can be used to tint eyelashes for them to read on camera.

• Taupe eye shadow can be applied as eyeliner to the upper and, if needed, lower lids.

• If taupe shadow is being used as liner, be sure to keep it a thin line, smudging it into the lash line as much as possible.

• Clean up and define brows, if necessary, but do not arch them – making them look like the feminine classic brow shape. If fair skinned the brows may not show up on camera, use a taupe eye shadow to fill in for color

• A light application of powder to set the base.

• Moisturize the lips if needed or use matte lip balm. Stay away from gloss.

All male make-ups must be very well blended and natural looking. To the viewer's eye, the male model's face should look cleaned up, but not made up. This make-up should not be obvious. Usually a male make-up, corrective or not, takes much less time to apply than a female model's make-up.

CHAPTER STUDY QUESTIONS

1. Are face-lifts used only for mature people?

2. How many parts are face-lifts composed of ?

3. What part of the face-lift is attached to the skin?

4. The link is made out of what type of material?

5. What does the fastener do?

6. Name the two types of face-lifts?

7. What are the advantages to over the counter face-lifts?

8. What is used to attach the leading edge to the skin?

9. How is the leading edge hidden ?

10. What is used to remove the leading edge?

CHAPTER 15

THE VARYING MEDIUMS

To utilize the skills of make-up artistry to the fullest we must have an understanding of how the make-up applications correspond with varying mediums we encounter as make-up artists. There are five general mediums, film, tape, print, stage and society. We say general mediums because each medium has a variety of choices, such as: film can be 35mm or 70mm, tape can be standard videotape (analog), or it might be digital or even "the always feared" High Definition tape.

Each of the varying mediums has differences in visual presentation. Each are critical in terms of how the make-up translates to screen or how it is seen by the viewer; for example, the larger an image is the more critical every detail becomes.

THE MEDIUMS

SOCIETY

Society make-up is usually the most critical due to its proximity to the viewer. This kind of make-up is typically done for public appearances, as well as for everyday wear. Since we see three dimensionally, society make-up must stand up to close examination and care has to be taken with the heaviness of it's application. Additionally, the make-up must look good in many different lighting conditions.

PRINT

Print make-up is not as critical as a society make-up but it represents the next closest thing to seeing a make-up in person. Print is an image frozen in time, meaning it is one frame of film not moving. The viewer can inspect the print very closely for an extended period of time if so desired. Print can be shot on a large format film negative, which captures every detail, or it may be shot with a digital camera, that produces a huge format image, usually 11x14 or larger, and which also shows a great amount of detail. In this medium the image is two-dimensional.

FILM

Film is next on our list of mediums. Film is less critical than tape due to its size. Because film is projected onto a screen it tends to create some diffusion as the light travels through the atmosphere. The film running through the projector also helps to soften the image, however due to the image's size you tend to see more detail. This too is a two-dimensional image.

TAPE

Tape is less critical than film for two simple reasons. First is its size in comparison to film. Second, is the way the image is recorded. Traditional tape is made up of an electronic image, which means the image on a monitor consists of many pixels that are assigned a color by the tape. The colors the tape assigns are limited to the number of colors the camera has in memory, so sometimes your red lip color may come out a different shade of orange when you see it played back. The lighting is usually washing the set, so it can be quite harsh on the performers. Most often the image is viewed on a smaller screen, such as a television.

STAGE

The make-up we do for stage needs to be balanced for the varying distances of the audience. Lighting conditions are usually pretty strong and the make-up must project through them. Make-ups for stage are exaggerated much more so than other mediums, primarily because they are character driven.

Note: The gap with two of the mediums (film and tape) is becoming closer all the time. Tape is getting a wider selection of colors, and digital is approaching film quality very rapidly.

THE MAKE-UP

SOCIETY

Society make-up requires that you develop a very keen and critical eye for perfection. Base matching and blending, well groomed eyebrows, even applications of eye shadow, smooth defined eyeliner, softly colored cheeks and well defined lip color applications are all a very important part of the process used in society make-up. This same eye for detail is carried over into all of the other mediums with varying differences applied to each medium.

PRINT

Remembering the frozen in time theory of the print medium, it is important to take time to carefully blend and check your application as you build the make-up to its completion.

Print make-up may be broken down into Color Photography and Black and White Photography. Both require extreme precision and blending in the applications. The color theory that was discussed in previous chapters applies to Color Photography as well. Defining specifics to print are as follows:

Various bases may be used in photography make-up including cream, liquid, and dual finish.

Creams may be used for print however, in some cases, you'll want to apply with a light touch and/or dilute them with moisturizer, a damp sponge or base thinner. This will give a sheerer application of the base. If the model's skin is more textured or pigmented, cream base would be the best choice. Be aware that cream make-up can appear heavy or caked in a photograph, especially on a mature face. On less than perfect skins, you may use liquid base all over, then carefully apply cream base over the imperfections and blend well with a fine brush. Cream bases tend to be water resistant.

Liquid foundation has a sheerer finish, especially if it is completely oil free. It looks more natural on the skin, so it is a good choice for outdoors, sporty, or beach looks. Application can be with a make-up sponge, brush, wet sea sponge, clean fingers or an airbrush depending on the coverage the artist wishes to achieve. Be aware that this base is not water resistant.

Dual-finish is packaged in compact form, and may have a wet to dry application. In this case, coverage can be adjusted by the amount of water used. A dryer sponge will allow for more coverage; a wetter sponge sheerer coverage. This make-up's finish tends to look a bit powdery on the skin, and in many cases will require less powder over it.

Powder application in print is crucial to the final look of your make-up. Too much powder will take away the natural translucency or glow of the skin, depending on the look you wish to achieve for the photograph; apply sparingly. Begin your powder application with a brush and a light touch, and then build as needed to create a more matte finish if desired. If too much powder is applied you can bring back the natural glow with a light misting of water on the skin. Be careful when applying powder around the eyes, as it will tend to collect in lines and wrinkles.

Color glow is important in color photography, as it can make or break the overall quality of warmth and vitality of the model. It tends to add softness and radiance to the face. This should be well blended without blotchiness.

Once again, blending is extremely important in the print medium, so take care to create soft edges on cheek color and eye shadows, unless it is a fashion or character look requiring a hard edge. The make-up should be completed as any other make-up, keeping in mind the medium in which you're working.

Black and white photography follows much of what was instructed in color photography, such as accuracy in details, and nearest to perfection in application. In black and white photography colors translate into shades of gray, as well as black and white, and may be lighter or darker on black and white film than they appear to the naked eye.

It differs in that you can't use color to soften or give glow to the skin, and contours become much more important as they create areas of highlight and shadow, giving dimension to the face. What looks strange to the natural eye in color has the ability to translate into black and white, as a beautiful make-up. For example, in a fashion black and white application, it is possible to actually use black eye shadow and lipstick and taupe (a "brown" that has a very "blue" undertone) as cheek color. This would look ridiculous to the naked eye! In black and white it simply becomes a very true black which, next to a pale skin tone, creates a beautiful, edgy contrast and a very pleasing photo.

It is important to understand how colors will translate into black and white. This is typically difficult for most people to automatically imagine because we see in color, therefore it must be taught. Every color used in black and white photography translates into various shades of gray, black or white.

Warm and cool colors—It is crucial to be able to see beyond color depth and into undertones of each true color. In black and white photography warm colors will appear as lighter shades of gray, and cool undertones will appear darker. For example, when looking at a brown eye shadow, note if its undertone is cool or warm. In other words, does it have more yellow or blue in its makeup? If it is a warm brown, it will translate lighter or more neutral on black and white film. If it is a cool brown, it will appear as a darker shade of gray, and look less natural.

When doing headshots, or any other black and white shoot that will require a more natural look, it is safer to stay with warmer tones. Colors used will not matter; as long as the undertone is warm, it will translate into a natural make-up.

For a black and white fashion shoot, or an application that calls for a more made-up look, colors that contain a blue undertone will help to achieve this. This can be any cool color, however the most obvious would be various shades of blues, charcoals and violets/purples.

Cheek colors that have warm undertones tend to disappear on black and white film. Here is a rare example of when you may use warm tones on the eye and lip treatments (such as peach, which will go to a very almost non-existent pale shade of gray), and mix with a cool toned (pink) cheek color. You may think you've applied enough blush, but be sure to check the Polaroid, as you may need to layer on more while on-set.

Similarly, with lip color, warm tones will create a very natural look in black and white, so if your make-up requires a bit more lip definition, you will want to use a lip color with a bluer undertone. (Typically in pinks) This will simply translate to a deeper shade of gray. Don't be fooled by reds! Again, look for the undertone. An orange-red (warmer) will become a more medium shade of gray, whereas a blue-red has the ability to look a very dark shade of gray and can sometimes appear almost black.

Foundation application is paramount in black and white, as any texture, discoloration or imperfection will be emphasized in the absence of color. Texture is highlight and shadow, and since there is no color to distract the viewer, the shadows will become more apparent. Pimples will become gray spots unless covered properly. Under eye circles have blue undertones and, therefore, have the ability to become very pronounced on black and white film. Careful attention should be taken with coverage. Shadows in the corners of the lips and around the nostrils can also become very pronounced and may need extra coverage. Glossy skin or lips are discouraged in natural applications of black and white make-up as they will create hot spots, or areas that become highlights; they will reflect the key light and will appear as white spots.

FILM

Unlike other mediums, in film we rarely adjust the base for the medium; we adjust it for the actor. (i.e. does the performer have good skin that requires less base or more texture that needs additional base to smooth it out); by comparison, in film the base application may be lighter than tape. Highlights and Shadows can be more subtle. You may choose a powder highlight and shadow instead of a cream. Lighter amounts of powder should be used. Sometimes, depending on the period or look of the movie, the actors may or may not need to appear matte. In a film make-up the eyes, lips and cheeks are character driven. Character driven means: what is the look according to the script, the actor, the make-up artist, the director, and the producer. Make-up needs to be applied to all exposed skin. Blending is very important as in all mediums

TAPE

Tape is typically used for game shows, soap operas, live shows and the news. Tape is generally more forgiving than film and print. There is less resolution with tape; therefore, tape is not as crisp as film. The result is more diffused to the viewer. Generally the image is in motion and viewed by the audience in a small format such as television.

Lighting is focused on the set rather than the actor Close-ups are less critical than on film due to diffused results. The base application, highlights and shadows are generally heavier in tape than in film, usually due to intensity of the lighting. Powder is heavier in order

to achieve a more matte finish. Cheek color may be heavier with attention given to finely blended edges. All exposed skin, such as the neck, hands and ears, requires make-up. It is recommended that you stay away from any products that contain glitter, iridescence or shimmer. Avoid using sparkly, shiny, or multi-colored lip color and be careful not to make the lips too dry. This is generally a fast paced make-up application. In tape each make-up artist may be responsible for multiple actors. Blending is very important to this application

STAGE

Stage make-up is often done by the actor. There may be a make-up artist who designs the looks and then shows the actors how to apply them. Other times the make-up artist stays with the theater company and is responsible for the make-up application. The stage make-up application is entirely character driven. Stage make-up is a very exaggerated make-up that must be seen from a distance. Cream bases and colored cream products, with a heavy application of powder to set the make-up, are generally the products of choice for the stage.

MUSIC VIDEO

In addition to the five general mediums covered there is make-up for Music Video. This is a creative world where a lot of "out of the ordinary" looks may be appropriate; eyes, lips, body painting. As in every medium, attention to detail must be followed. Extreme close-ups, creative photography, and unconventional shots are aspects of music videos. In a music video it is not uncommon to be filmed or taped, sometimes at the same time, so the make-up needs to translate well to each. Due to the amount of time it takes to complete a music video the make-up needs to hold up under extreme conditions, such as, perspiration, lights, and late nights. This make-up technique holds up well for all skin types, as it covers and evens out skin with texture. Music Videos are a perfect medium for edgier, funkier or more extreme make-up.

PACKING YOUR SET BAG

The set bag is an extension of your kit, used to carry the items you will need to do touch-ups on the actors while on set/location. The set is where the camera is, regardless of the medium. Packing or loading your set bag properly is important in keeping the make-up artist mobile and prepared.

TOOLS AND SUPPLIES

Because the set bag is a scaled down version of your kit it can be personalized to suit your needs. Packing small and compact is the key to having a fully stocked

set bag. What you keep in the set bag will change for each actor's needs.

Here is a list of items you might consider having with you on set.

1. Japonesque foundation/lipstick palette -Will hold multiple shades of lip color.

2. Small zip lock bags - Label the bag with talent's name, using a permanent marker, then place talent's

sponge, powder puff, and other personal grooming items in the baggie, then into the set bag. This is especially important when you are on set, touching up more than one talent.

3. Wax paper palettes - Blend the actor's base on the paper palette, rather than the metal palettes for the convenience of folding the palette and placing it in the labeled baggie. This gives the artist the perfectly blended base that may be required for touch up.

4. Comb/brush: A small roll of various combs and brushes works well for on-set touch-ups.

5. Hair spray/hair balm: Whatever products were used on the talent should be in your set bag. Consider using small sizes to conserve space in your set bag.

6. Make-up Remover Towelettes: Used to remove unwanted make-up.

7. Sponges: Loaded with the talent's base for quick touch-ups. Clean sponges in case you need them.

8. Powder puff: The one used in the original make-up application. Should be re-loaded with the talent's powder, ready for a touch-up.

9. Small eye shadow palette: with the colors used in the original application

10. Small cheek color/blush palette: with the colors used in the original application

11. Make-up brushes: Any brushes you will need for touch-up, such as a lip brush (loaded), eye shadow brushes, and a cheek color brush.

12. Powder: Whatever shade(s) were used in the original application. to re-load the puff as needed.

13. Alcohol/Hand Sanitizer: To keep items and hands bacteria free.

14. Polaroid Camera: To record the work for make-up continuity.

15. Polaroid Film: For the camera, an extra roll kept in the set bag is recommended.

16. Hole punch: To punch a hole in the continuity shots.

17. Metal ring: To place continuity shots on, and to attach to the set bag allowing easy access.

18. Spray water: Preferably a pressurized can of water. For clean up and if the talent needs to look sweaty.

19. Cotton Swabs: Store in a small container, use for the removal of small flaws, blending, or applying make-up.

20. Tissue: Used to pat excess sweat or oil from the face; also used for clean up.

21. Hand Mirror: In case you need the view of the make-up in a mirror while on-set.

22. Permanent Marker: To mark the talent's individual bags containing puffs, sponges etc.

23. Camouflage palette: For imperfections that may need to be maintained throughout the shoot.

Generally there will be certain items that will stay in your set bag at all times, such as: eye drops, flashlight, straws, small first aid kit, umbrella, breath mints or spray, safety pins, lubricating eye drops, sunscreen, bug spray, lip moisturizer, hand lotion, double sided tape, nail kit, file, clear polish, cuticle scissors, styptic stick, and earplugs.

Other items will change based on who you need to touch-up. Other items you may want to purchase include a set chair, portable lighted table, notebook, pen, highlighter and Thomas Guide. Build your kit/set bag as the need arises.

CHAPTER STUDY QUESTIONS

1. There are how many general mediums?

2. Which of the mediums is the most critical?

3. Which of the mediums is the least critical?

4. What role does texture play in black and white photography?

5. Is tape more or less forgiving than film?

6. In print, what is frozen in time?

7. In film, what softens the image?

8. What medium is often viewed on a small screen?

9. Stage make-up is entirely driven by what?

10. What type of make-up should be avoided in tape?

CHAPTER 16

AIRBRUSH

The basic concepts of operating an airbrush for use in a beauty make-up application give the make-up artist an understanding of the mechanical workings and breakdown of the airbrush. With the basic concepts you are about to learn, and a little practice, you too can become a proficient artist with the airbrush.

AIRBRUSH BASICS

Most airbrushes are designed to allow water-based paints, oils, adhesives, enamels, acrylics and make-ups to flow through them. Any free-flowing material with the consistency of milk may be sprayed through an airbrush.

Before we explain how to use the airbrush, we should first tell you how the tool works. An airbrush is a small metal tool attached to a hose, which is then connected to a source for air such as a compressor. There is a small button or trigger on the airbrush that allows us to release air from the tool. The air moves past a small opening at the tip of the tool, creates a vacuum, and draws the make-up into the air stream. The air and the make-up are shot from the tool towards whatever one is painting.

The two types of airbrushes that we will be discussing will be the single-action and the double-action airbrush. Most manufacturers of airbrushes make both styles plus a few more. The term single action refers to the trigger motion on the airbrush. The trigger only has one function; when it is pressed down both make-up and air are released from the tool. There is usually some other knob or screw on the airbrush, which allows you to set the amount of make-up that will spray out when you press the trigger. Double action also refers to the motion of the trigger. By pressing down on the trigger, air is released from the tool, by pulling back on the trigger you allow paint to mix with the air and spray from the tool.

Some airbrushes come with interchangeable parts to adjust the spray pattern and for the viscosity of the fluid. Thicker fluids require a larger nozzle and more pressure. Pattern size is determined by the size of the nozzle or tip of the airbrush and the distance the airbrush is held from the painting surface.

Single-action airbrushes are extremely durable and will allow almost anything to be sprayed through them. Additionally, they are very easy to clean and maintain, as well as simple to operate. The double-action airbrush is the workhorse of the industry and is used by a large number of artists because of its versatility. Its uses range from painting animatronics skins to applying body make-up. This airbrush is a little more difficult to use because it requires a little more hand-eye coordination. Keep your airbrush clean and in good working order. Follow the manufacturer's instructions that come with the airbrush, and it will become a vital tool in your make-up kit.

AIR SUPPLY

In order for an airbrush to work, it requires air to be pushed though it. There are a wide variety of ways of providing air to your airbrush. The most common is a compressor, but the challenge is finding the right one for you.

The first option is a compressor motor. These are generally inexpensive; however, they do not supply an even airflow and can be quite noisy.

The next option is a compressor with a tank attached. The benefit of this type is an even airflow and a motor that shuts off once the tank is full; the motor restarts only to refill the tank. This type of a compressor is still noisy when the motor is on.

The third option is a silent compressor, which has a motor and a tank. This motor is insulated and runs much quieter than its predecessors. However, this type of compressor is very expensive. It is as much as three to four times more than a standard compressor.

A fourth option is the use of carbon dioxide gas. Though carbon dioxide isn't technically air, art stores carry a carbon dioxide in spray paint size cans. You may also purchase carbon dioxide canisters from a welding supply, which will last much longer and can be refilled. Canisters come in several sizes: 10-lb., 20-lb., and some suppliers have even larger sizes; 10-lb. tanks will typically last about 10 hours of moderate spraying and a 20-lb. tank will last about 20 hours.

MAINTENANCE

Before laying your airbrush aside, even for a short period, empty it of all color and run water through it or the proper solvent for the medium you are using. There will be times when product will dry inside the airbrush and begin to clog it. The performance of the airbrush will be greatly affected if it is not cleaned. To thoroughly clean the airbrush, you must dismantle it. Refer to the diagrams of each airbrush to ensure proper disassembly and assembly. With the airbrush completely taken apart, you will be able to thoroughly clean every portion of it.

OPERATING THE AIRBRUSH

There are three movements that the beginner needs to become familiar with. Hold the airbrush so the tip of the forefinger rests on the button that activates the airflow. Press down on the button to start air flowing through the brush. For a double-action airbrush, pulling back on the button will start the flow of product. Next, move your hand to the right and left, and up and down.

The distance the tip of the airbrush is from the work surface will vary the size of the spray pattern. The further away you are, the wider the spray pattern, the closer you are to the surface, the thinner the line. Build up your colors gradually. Too much product, or a surface that is overly wet, will start to run.

AIRBRUSH EXERCISES

Here are some simple lessons we recommend trying to enable you to gain basic control of the airbrush. The following lessons are designed to be done on paper, then on the skin, and should be carried out in the fashion described.

EXERCISE 1

This exercise is designed to give you some basic control over the airbrush. We will use the process of making dots; this activity will help to gain control. Start out on paper before moving to skin and use a water-based make-up for easy clean up. To familiarize yourself with the feel and the functions of the airbrush, practice spraying air from the tool. Now, hold the airbrush about one inch from the paper, begin spraying air, and then slowly pull back on the trigger to introduce make-up. Practice this process until you are able to place dots accurately, without spraying too much make-up onto the paper. If you pull back on the trigger too far make-up will pool in one spot, creating a puddle. Next, adjust the size of the dots and the intensity of the dots. To accomplish this you will have to allow more make-up to spray out of the airbrush and you will need to increase the distance between the airbrush and the surface you are painting. Once you have mastered this skill you will be able to place color wherever you need it, and in any quantity.

EXERCISE 2

This exercise will enable you to evenly apply make-up with the airbrush, as well as blend color from one area to another. When using an airbrush for a make-up application, often times we are applying base to an actor's face, or creating an even skin tone over an entire body. Again, start out on paper before trying this on skin. White paper will show the areas where you need more coverage. Practice moving the airbrush left and right over the paper. Make sure you move your hand right to left before releasing any color. Otherwise, where you begin and end your move will cause the coverage to be heavier than in the middle,

creating spots at the beginning and end of your move. Another technique to achieve the same result, is working in a circular motion with the airbrush to create a smooth, even coverage over a large area. The final result should be a thin, even application of color without any puddles.

EXERCISE 3

The final exercise is meant to help you apply color in layers. Start by spraying a thin application of color in a horizontal line about two inches in height. Next, spray another horizontal line with the same thickness of color about one inch in height, but this time overlap the previous line, covering the bottom half of the first line. Finally, do a third line, again the same thickness of color, but only half an inch thick. The result should be a nice gradation of color from light on top to dark on the bottom.

Repeating these exercises over and over, first on paper then on skin, will give you the skills and confidence to use the airbrush in a beauty make-up environment. This is just the beginning of your efforts to use the airbrush professionally. The airbrush can be used to apply body make-up or beauty make-up. For beauty make-up, use the airbrush when applying the base, the highlights under the eyes, the cheekbone shadow, the jaw line shadow, and when applying cheek color to the top of the cheekbone.

CHAPTER STUDY QUESTIONS

1. What consistency is best for flowing liquid through the airbrush?

2. Airbrushes may be single or double-action?

3. The size of the nozzle determines what?

4. Describe a good technique of creating a smooth, even coverage over a large area.

5. When would we use an airbrush in doing a make-up application?

6. What is used to provide the air to the airbrush?

7. Why is it important to clean the airbrush after each use?

8. What will vary the size of the spray pattern?

9. Too much product on the surface will do what?

10. Will the airbrush create only a fine line?

CHAPTER 17

BODY MAKE-UP

Body make-up introduces a larger canvas for the make-up artist. With this comes many choices in equipment, tools and products that are available for applying make-up to the body.

INTRODUCTION

Any make-up applied to the body is generally defined as body make-up and, on occasion, as body painting. A body make-up may mean simply evening out skin tones or, taken to the extreme, a fantasy type application. Whatever the desired look, there are several methods available.

Not only are there choices in application method, there are choices in product as well: liquid foundation/base applied either by a make-up sponge or shot through an airbrush, water-based or oil-free cake make-up applied with a sea sponge. Whatever the choice, the goal is to achieve an even application.

Some liquid make-up works well in the airbrush while others, perhaps, have too long, or not long enough, drying time.

Experimentation with the various products on different skin types is recommended to obtain the desired results.

AIRBRUSH AND BEAUTY MAKE-UP

The Airbrush can be a wonderful addition to the make-up artist's kit, but should be viewed as just that, an addition not a replacement; it certainly can be a useful tool when it comes to producing an even coverage over larger areas, when laying down a base, or, for example, when doing a body make-up application. (It can be a viable tool in creating highlights and shadows.)

For fine detail work such as an eyeliner application a steady hand and a make-up brush will yield the best results.

When using the airbrush for base or foundation on the face, or when applying body make-up (torso, arms, legs, etc.), the make-up chosen will most likely need to be thinned to allow the product to flow through the airbrush freely.

Liquid make-ups can be very different from one cosmetic manufacturer to the next. Experimenting with the different product lines is recommended, so that the make-up artist may get a feel for what works best to achieve the desired look.

Remember that the airbrush should be considered an addition to the make-up artist's kit and not a replacement tool.

SPONGE APPLICATION

LIQUID
Liquid make-up may also be applied with a traditional make-up sponge. This generally will take longer than an application applied with the airbrush; therefore, it's use is recommended for smaller areas of application, such as the hands or chest.

This method will have a sheer coverage and may need to be powdered afterwards.

CAKE
Cake make-up has been around for many years and, when it comes to body make-up, still yields great results.

Applied with a sea-sponge or today's manufactured sea-sponge this application can appear flawless.

The use of water is necessary for this method. The amount of water is important when using cake make-up. It is best to wring out the dampened sponge before adding the make-up to the sponge. Add more water to the sponge as necessary.

This product dries quickly and will not need to be powdered. This method works well for small or large areas, and the coverage is medium to heavy with a matte finish.

CHAPTER STUDY QUESTIONS

1. What types of foundation may be used for body make-up?

2. When working with a sponge what type of make-up would you choose?

3. A sea sponge is used with what type of make-up?

4. Which body make-up will not need to be powdered?

5. What is the purpose of using a body make-up?

6. Which tool will work well to create highlights and shadows?

CHAPTER 18
OUTSIDE THE BOX

Continuing the educational process involves opening the mind and eyes of make-up artists in the way they approach the make-up application. In other words, "thinking outside the box" or not allowing themselves to get locked into one way of doing make-up.

THE CREATIVE PROCESS

This chapter is dedicated to taking the make-up application to the next level. In doing this, the make-up artist will need to expand the way he or she looks at the make-up application.

With the majority of beauty make-up applications requiring a natural or "no-make-up" make-up look, this is an opportunity to elevate the imagination.

Not every make-up done will have all aspects or contain all of the elements previously discussed. As an example, not every make-up will require eye liner; not every make-up will need concealer.

Remember that make-up is applied as necessary, or as desired by the make-up artist to achieve a vision.

That vision can be endless, with the make-up artist limited only by his or her imagination. How creative a make-up is, is solely dependent upon the creativity of the make-up artist. After all, applying make-up is an art.

There are guidelines that make the process a combination of technique and art, such as the theory of highlights and shadow. These guidelines may still be applied with expanded vision.

There are several wonderful books that help to open the creativeness within all of us. These books are not about make-up but rather about opening up the creative aspects of ourselves. *The Artist's Way* by Julia Cameron and *Drawing on the Right Side of the Brain* by Betty Edwards are just two of the books that are recommended reading. Both of these may also be found on-line.

To be a great make-up artist one must tap into and explore his or her own creativity.

CHOICES

Color is a wonderful way to further the creative process and will ultimately enhance the make-up. Also to be considered are the variety of product choices that are available today, creams, powder, gels, matte or iridescent, the choices are vast.

The following are suggestions that may be used separately or in combination:

Base application may remain as a natural make-up application. This represents preparing the canvas (the face) for the make-up artist. How, if at all, this make-up will be seen on camera will determine the base application.

Eyebrows may be neutral or enhanced with a different shade (lighter or darker).

Eye shadow application allows the artist more freedom. This is an area considered to be a playground for the make-up artist. The choices are endless, from the positioning of the eye shadow to how bright or muted the color choice may be.

Eye liner is similar in its range of choices to eye shadow. The make-up artist needs to maintain lift to the eye. Liners can be smudged and/or bright.

Lashes can use brighter shades of mascara and several more coats than in natural make-up applications.

Lashes may also be enhanced by the use of false lashes. Strip or individual, natural or brightly colored, are the make-up artist's choices. Use a few or many.

Cheeks overall can have more color or iridescence.

Lips can have splashes of highlight.

Whatever the choices, experimenting and practicing with different products on many different faces will aid make-up artists in perfecting their craft.

SUGGESTIONS

FOUNDATION
Following the guidelines from the Base and Corrective Make-up chapter, apply and powder.

EYEBROWS
Following the guidelines from the Eyebrow chapter, shape and/or fill in the eyebrows.

EYE SHADOW
Examples
Combine matte shadows with iridescent shadows within the same hues or complementary shades. Such as:

Color Combination 1:
Apply a light soft green shade to the upper lid and a metallic medium green shade to the fold. Apply a light cream shade under the eyebrow.

Color Combination 2:
Apply a golden yellow shade to the upper lid and a deep forest green shade to the fold.
Apply a soft light pink shade under the eyebrow.

Color Combination 3:
Apply a deep rich metallic purple to the upper lid and a muted slate blue-gray shade to the fold. Apply a soft light pink shade or a light cream shade under the eyebrow.

Color Combination 4:
Apply a metallic copper shade to the upper lid and a violet plum shade to the fold.
Apply a soft light pink shade under the eyebrow.

Color Combination 5:
Apply a pink-coral shade to the upper lid and a deep golden sand shade to the fold.
Apply a soft light pink shade under the eyebrow.

Examples
Choose primarily iridescent colors, such as:

Color Combination 1:
Apply a deep golden sand shade to the upper lid and a vibrant golden green to the fold.
Apply a light cream shade under the eyebrow.

Color Combination 2:
Apply a soft light pink shade to the upper lid and a deep rich metallic purple to the fold.
Apply a soft light pink shade under the eyebrow.

Color Combination 3:
Apply a golden yellow shade to the upper lid and a metallic medium green shade to the Fold. Apply a soft light pink shade under the Eyebrow.

Examples
Choose several different colors, combining matte and/or iridescent, such as:

Color Combination 1:
Apply three shades in any combination. Try alternating positions for different effects.

Color Combination 2:
Apply a golden yellow shade to the upper lid and under the eyebrow, and a deep rich metallic purple shade on the fold, blending the top and bottom edges into the golden yellow shade. Use black to deepen the edge of the fold.

Color Combination 3:
Apply a golden yellow shade to the upper lid and under the eyebrow on the fold, and a deep metallic sand shade over a rich vibrant orange shade. Blend edges.

EYE LINER
Example
Using the fashion or glamour Eye Liner positions smudge the edges to create a smoky, sultry look. For example, apply then smudge eye shadow.
Try these matte shades: black, a slate gray, a slate blue and rich dark sand.

Example
Using the Fashion Eye Liner position to create a trendy look. For example, apply then smudge eye shadow in these vibrant shades: metallic green, deep rich metallic purple, deep metallic peacock blue, metallic turquoise and rich deep green.

Example
Layer a light gray, a slate gray and black for a smoked eye shadow treatment with dimension.

LASHES
Build up with several coats of mascara. Try an eggplant, plum or burgundy shade.

CHEEKS
Try rich vibrant colors such as orange peach, then lightly dust with a soft iridescent pink.

LIPS
Example
For dark, rich, lips use lip liner that is one to two shades darker than the lip color. Add dots of a gold shimmer to the upper lip just below the peaks of the Cupid's Bow and in the center of the lower lip. A gold shimmer, being a highlight, will pull those areas of the lip forward for a full, pouty look.

Example
For light lips use lip liner that is the same shade as the lip color. Add dots of a silver shimmer to the upper lip just below the peaks of the Cupid's Bow, and in the center of the lower lip.

Try a light eye treatment with dark lips or a dark eye treatment with light lips. Whatever the choices or combinations, the art of make-up is a creative process.

CHAPTER 19

THE BUSINESS END

Apart from the actual make-up application, make-up artists need to be educated in other areas of the business. This includes knowing the industry terminology, understanding what the make-up artist's responsibilities are, and knowing how to maintain continuity throughout a project.

TERMINOLOGY

The following is a list of general industry terminology, primarily as it applies to film; however this may also apply to other mediums in varying degrees.

1. Make-up/Hair: Production Department (job category)

2. Department Head: most senior department managers. Productions with more than one shooting location at a time will have a department head supervise all key make-ups on location.

3. Key Make-up: 1st Asst. Make-up/Hair-Person usually selected by the key hair, make-up, or fashion stylist as their assistant. This individual has been identified by the key as fully capable of handling some or all aspects of a job.

4. Make-up: 2nd Asst. Make-up/Hair-Person who supports 1st make-up and key.

5. Day Checker: Person hired on a day labor basis, to work within the department. The Day Checker can be responsible for day players or background extras, depending upon the film and department head.

6. DP: Director of Photography.

7. 1st/2nd AD: Assistant Directors.

8. DGA Trainee: Director trainee approved by the Directors Guild of America

9. Gaffer: Head Electrician/Lighting Director.

10. Key Grip: Person responsible for the Grips department.

11. Dolly Grip: Person responsible for the dolly equipment to move camera.

12. Best Boy: 1st Asst to Gaffer & Key Grip – Person responsible for all equipment assigned to the production crew, both permanent equipment and expendables.

13. CGI (Computer Generated Imagery)- Photoshop for film.

14. Director: The person responsible for all the creative decisions on a production. This person makes the script or treatment a reality.

15. Executive Producer: The person who is responsible for overseeing a video, commercial, television or film project. The executive producer also hires the producer.

16. Production Coordinator: Person who is responsible for maintaining contact with and giving direction (per the producer) to the crew on a video, commercial, television or film project.

17. Production Manager: Person who is in charge of managing all aspects and all departments on a production.

18. Publicist: Person whose job it is to promote an individual, company or entity in the media.

19. Still Photographer: Photography of inanimate objects, as opposed to photography of people.

20. PA: Production Assistant: The person who is available to assist in all departments and all aspects of a production.

CONTINUITY

Webster's definition describes continuity as: the state or quality of being continuous, film smooth, and matching transitions from one shot or sequence to the next.

When working as a make-up artist for film, commercial, television shows, or any project that requires continuous scenes, continuity becomes of the utmost importance.

Film is rarely shot in sequence. The last scene of a film may be shot on the first day of shooting and so on. The viewing audience rarely notices when one shot runs into another provided that the transition is a smooth one. One shot does not flow smoothly into the next. Shots edited together without continuity issues make for a scene the audience can view without distraction. It is the make-up artist's responsibility to prevent these breaks in continuity as it relates to make-up.

CONTINUITY PHOTOS

To ensure that continuity is taking place the make-up artist will need to record the make-up for each of the characters; this is done by taking a picture. Generally the Polaroid camera has been the industry standard. However, with the technical advances being made today, more and more people are using digital cameras to record their work. Whatever the method of choice, it is important that the work be recorded and documented.

CONTINUITY BOOK /CONTINUITY RING

Some make-up artists prefer to keep a three-ring binder with plastic sleeves, combined with sheets of paper for notes. This is called a continuity book. The plastic sleeves have pockets made to hold the photos and the remaining information is recorded on the notepaper. Another option is to use a metal ring to hold the photos. Labels are necessary for this method as well as a hole punch.

WHEN TO TAKE PHOTOS

When should the photo be taken? After the master shot is usually the best time to take a photo. The photo is being taken to enable the make-up artist to match shot for shot when necessary. The master is described as the first completed shot of a scene, which every shot from that scene will then be matched to. As an example, think of six people sitting around a dining room table having dinner. The camera is focused on all six people engaged in conversation. Once the Director and the Director of Photography are happy with the way it has been shot, that will be the master to which the following shots will be matched. The camera may then focus on perhaps two of the people talking, then focus down to each individual person. The same lines are being said; the same scene is being shot. It is how the camera is shooting the scene that makes the difference. Each time the artist must match to the master. If the photo was taken immediately after the make-up was completed, but the master is not shot shortly afterward, there is a chance that the make up may not look exactly like it did when it was first completed, interrupting the continuity.

CONTINUITY CHARTS

Written record of product usage. A complete written explanation of what products were used on each character, providing individual details in order to give direction to other artists, not just the key; also, to enable the artist to move easily from day to day when a production goes on for weeks, possibly months, etc. Continuity charts are especially helpful during pick-up shots. A pick-up shot may be done 6 or more months after the principle photography has wrapped.

MORE ABOUT CONTINUITY

It is ultimately the key's responsibility to make sure that continuity photos are being taken; whether the key takes them or designates another person within that department to do so. There should be someone from the make-up department on set at all times to do "touch-ups" ensuring the continuity of the make-up.

DOCUMENTING THE WORK

After taking the picture the make up artist will then need to label the picture, identifying:

- Who the character is

- What scene number it is

- What day or night in the script it is

On some occasions it may also be necessary to document the age of the character. This is especially helpful when the character portrays different ages throughout the film. When taking Polaroids this can be done on the white band that runs under the photo.

It may be necessary to document the instructions and products used to achieve the make-up desired. When using Polaroids this may be done using labels made for this purpose, which will then go on the back of the Polaroid.

FLASHING

There are several departments that take photos on a set, with Script, Wardrobe, Set Dressing, Make-up and Hair being amongst them. There are other departments that work on the set that don't need to take pictures, however they are aware of what taking pictures on set is all about. It is expected that the person using the camera will say, "Flashing" to alert the people around them that a flash is about to happen. This will alert crew that this a controlled flash and not a problem with lighting. Another reason to say "flashing" is to let others taking pictures know so that two people do not flash at the same time, possibly ruining the photos.

PRODUCTION RESPONSIBILITIES

As with every other department head you will need to break down the script for your department. In the breakdown you will have to determine what every look, for every character in each scene, will be. You will need to create a budget for materials used during the production. Likewise you will need to identify the scenes that require more assistance, and characters that need more time. Your final responsibility is to do this accurately to ensure your department does not run over in budget or time.

GENERAL INFORMATION

The following information is designed to help the make-up artist prepare for a number of situations. This will help to ensure professionalism and confidence.

MUSIC VIDEO

When doing a music video it is important to work with the director, to enable you to interpret the concept of the song or the talent. The make-up artist should be able to present the concepts with images from magazines and drawings. Familiarize yourself with the director's previous works.

• This medium can be a showcase for your work. Usually the artist will be trying to achieve a new look, which gives the artist the opportunity to try new products, techniques, etc.

• Concepts may change and often do. It is important to be flexible in order to accommodate the director and talent's request.

• It is the make-up artist's responsibility to be well prepared and organized in order to have talent completed when called to set.

• Ask questions of Production in order to allow yourself to be prepared; questions about the different shots, such as, interior or exterior shots, day or night, etc.

• Music videos usually consist of long hours. It is important that you be prepared in all aspects of the job including taking care of yourself.

AT THE PHOTO SHOOT

Even though a photo shoot can be a more casual environment, it is equally important that the make-up artist be just as prepared and professional.

The following is an overview of a typical day on a photo shoot:

• Be on time. Make sure you eat, get coffee, and set up before the model's call time.

• Speak to the photographer and/or art director about the look they want, the lighting, and when they want the model on set.

• Collaborate with the hair and wardrobe stylists on how much time they will need so you can adjust your timing accordingly and have the model on set on time. (In most cases, you are allowed more time on a print set to do make-up than on a video, television, or film shoot. Typically, 45 minutes to one hour is comfortably acceptable for make-up.)

• Ask if there is a layout available. (A layout is a hand sketched or computer generated drawing by the art director of the expected outcome of your photo shoot.) This will give you a concrete idea of what they want the model to look like when he/she is camera ready.

ON SET

• Pack the appropriate set bag.

• Stand behind the photographer while they are shooting to ensure that you are seeing the subject from his camera angle. Be sure not to get in his way or engage in unnecessary conversation!

• Polaroid's, or digital test images, will be taken first to make sure everything and everyone on set is ideally prepared for the shot. Look and listen! The photographer and agency/creative directors will have input and any adjustments to lighting, props and/or model will be made at this time.

• During shooting, if you need to step onto set an ideal time is between roll changes. Quietly tell the photographer and wait for his o.k. Be quick and efficient with touch-ups. When crossing in front of the lens say "crossing".

• If multiple changes to set and/or wardrobe are happening throughout the shoot day, ask if any adjustments need to be made to the make-up such as lip color, eye shadow intensity, or eyeliner.

• At the end of the shoot day, clean your area thoroughly, thank everyone and offer the model anything he/she may need to remove the make-up.

Keep in mind that a print set is much smaller, personal and less formal than a television studio or film set; however, all the same etiquette rules apply.

ON LOCATION

This means you will be shooting in an area away from the photography studio. You may be indoors or out—such as at a park or beach.

• Bring your make-up chair if needed. There are no "grip trucks" on a print shoot, so don't assume a chair will be provided for you.

• Remember you may not be doing make-up in ideal situations. At times, your make-up box may be on the ground (bring towels), you may be out in the desert without a motor home to work in, or doing make-up off of the tailgate of a truck. When outdoors, most of the time you will not have a mirror to work from. (No whining allowed.)

• Ask for what you need. If you are out in the sun and need a scrim set up for you to block the direct sunlight on the model, ask the assistant if they will kindly set one up for you. If you are in a dark bathroom at an indoor location, or required to work in fluorescent light, ask if a better light can be spared and set up for you.

• Bring snacks. There is generally no craft service, and although drinks/water will usually be provided, there may not be any food available until designated lunch/dinner breaks.

• Have baby wipes/hand sanitizer accessible, as a bathroom may not be easily or quickly available for frequent hand washings.

• Layer your clothing so you are prepared for any weather conditions or changes, and bring plenty of sunscreen and/or a hat and sunglasses.

PRINT FORMATS

There are several formats that photographers use. This may be personal preference, or for professional reasons.

• 8X10 AND 4X5: very large formats in which sheets of film are used that have been pre-loaded into holders that are inserted into the top of the camera upside-down. These produce very large negatives that will enlarge without losing any detail. (In fact, providing incredible detail—great for billboards.)

• 2 1/4: The most popular format used in advertising photography. Usually Hasselblad (German) cameras are used and the rolls of film are loaded into camera backs, which are then attached to the back of the camera. This produces a large square negative, and there are 20 shots per roll of film. This format produces a negative, which is ideal for enlarging to 8x10 or 11x14 size photographs without losing detail.

• 35 mm: Used a lot for outdoor fashion photography, weddings, and catalogs. Produces a small negative that is great for enlarging up to 8x10 without losing detail. It is difficult to crop in and enlarge parts of this size negative (such as taking a full-length shot and trying to just print a headshot out of it) because you will lose too much detail and the image will be grainy. Note: This changes when working with 35 mm professional digital equipment, as digital produces amazing clarity, and images are saved directly to disk and/or hard drive; so you can immediately retouch, color correct and print any size from a digital capture.

FILM FOR DEVELOPING PRINT

• Print size: You may order portfolio prints in 8x10, 9x12, or 11x14, depending on the size of your portfolio. Most professional portfolios these days are either 9x12 (a size that originated in Europe with modeling agencies), or 11x14. Most labs will have prices available for all three sizes; however, some do not offer 9x12. You may still order a 9x12 print, (just ask them to print you a 9x12 image on 11x14 paper, and then crop the borders); you will be charged for an 11x14 print, however.

• Matte or glossy? Matte finish is a sort of pearl look, but no shine. Glossy is a smooth paper with a very shiny surface. Note that glossy prints will fingerprint easily.

• Cropping instructions: You should have an idea of how you want to crop your image. You will offer the lab a guideline by using a grease pencil to outline your desired image on the proof/contact sheet. Your initial crop will be approximate, since the printing machines have linear perimeters. Due to this fact, you will be given a special cropper that will be adjusted for your print size; you must use this for marking your final print borders. Ask for a full bleed if you want your print to have no borders. If you do want borders, they will usually be black on color prints, and white on black and white prints. (You may ask for white borders on your color print, but there is an extra charge.)

• Color Instructions: For color photos, you may instruct the lab to print with good skin tones and to print for make-up. Also, if you notice that the skin tone could be a bit warmer, to ensure that your make-up work looks the best it can, (for example, if it was shot using outdoor available light and it was an overcast day) you can have the lab add yellow or red to the final print. (If it is too warm, blue will correct this.) Ask for their color sample gels, which you can lay over the contact sheet to see what these color additions will look like. In addition, if you notice that an area of the photo has a hot spot, you can ask for it to be dodged in the printing process. (They will take the area down) Conversely, if an area is dark and you wish for it to be lightened, instruct them to "burn" that area and they will open it up (lighten it) for you. They can do this without affecting the entire print.

• Digital Images: You should bring your disk or CD to a lab that offers digital prints. (Not all do yet) Have your retouching and color corrections (Photoshop) already done. All you will have to do then is give print size and desired crop.

• Photo retouching can be done on the prints themselves (by hand), but it is quite expensive and may sometimes take up to a week or more. Also, keep in mind that your print will be sprayed with a fixative (so the retouching paints used are secure), which will create an extremely matte finish.

OTHER PRINT TERMINOLOGY

Flopping: If your subject is facing left on the negative, and you want them facing right on your final print, the image is "flopped" (give this instruction when ordering)

Cross Process or C-41: A type of color film processed in the lab with chemicals that "tweak" the colors. They become more vivid and contrast-y, almost electric looking. This process was popular several years ago and has not yet made resurgence into mainstream editorial or advertising photography.

Wide-angle or fisheye: A lens used by the photographer to comically distort the subject, creating the look of a large head on a small body.

Agency: On an advertising photo shoot, the ad agency is the group who hires the photographer (his/her client). There are usually at least two people on the shoot who are from the agency and they give the photographer final image approval on Polaroids and film. They also may give you make-up instructions and/or final approval on the model before they go out on set.

Art Director: This person is typically with the agency or hired by the agency to create an ad idea (or magazine layout). They focus on making sure the images created by the photographer mimic their client's needs and desired final outcome.

Tear sheet: A tear sheet is a photo or group of photos that has been torn out of a magazine.

Promo card: Short for promotional card, this is usually a 6x8 size printed card that has select photos of your work arranged on it and is sent/given out to potential clients. This is an important factor in your marketing process for print work.

PORTFOLIO

In print, your portfolio is your resume. Sometimes you are required to drop it off for viewing without even meeting your potential client. It should always be clean, orderly, and professional—and ready to go out at a moment's notice. Clean the pages periodically to keep them free of dust and fingerprints. Check the photos after they have been viewed to straighten any that may have floated askew inside the sheet protectors. At least once per year you will need to replace the pages, as they become scratched and "muddy" looking

after repeated viewing. Keep it in a cool place that is not exposed to the sun, as heat will damage the pages. You may purchase the common black leather portfolio, or choose your own design. If you choose a leather book, periodically clean it with leather cleaner and protect it with a non-oily leather moisturizer. Make sure you have your name embossed on the cover, or purchase a nameplate at a trophy store, which can easily be affixed to the cover.

LIGHTING

Lighting is an art in itself and probably beyond the scope of this course. We suggest a college lighting course to better understand the details of color temperature, corrective color filters, and lighting instruments. Also, most photography courses get more detailed with lighting terminology.

Lighting is of critical importance in film, video, and print. For print specifically, the primary need-to-know aspects of lighting are as follows:

LIGHTING POSITIONS
There are four main lighting positions.
Key Light—The key light is the main source of illumination on set and/or the subject and usually the brightest light on the set as well.

Fill light—This light illuminates one or both sides of the model, filling areas that the key light leaves in shadow. It softens the harshness of the key light.

The Hair Light or Rim Light—This light is placed above and sometimes slightly behind the model. It will illuminate the hair, separating the model from the background, and bring detail and true color to the hair.

Back Light—The backlight illuminates everything behind the model. It also allows for more separation from the background.

Intensity refers to the bright or dim quality of the lighting. After all the lights have been placed, the photographer or assistant will use a light meter to balance the proper intensity and adjust his/her shutter speed and F-stop accordingly. At this point, a light may be brightened, a filter may be placed in front of a light to dim the intensity, the duration of the flash may be adjusted, and/or a color gel may be placed over a light to warm the skin tone of the subject or otherwise adjust the overall color of the set.

If the intensity is extremely bright, it can possibly wash out features, shadows, and colors, which may require more base coverage, color depth, and contouring in the make-up application.

Conversely, if the light intensity is very low or dim it tends to soften the details and you may need to adjust the make-up by adding more definition and color intensity.

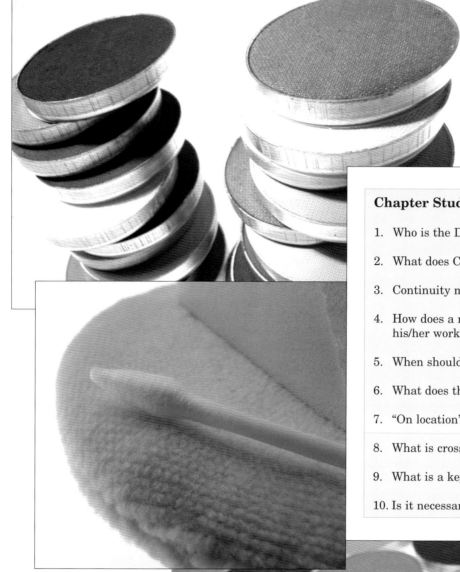

Chapter Study Questions

1. Who is the D.P?

2. What does CGI stand for?

3. Continuity means what?

4. How does a make-up artist document his/her work?

5. When should a continuity shot be taken?

6. What does the term "flashing" mean?

7. "On location" means what?

8. What is cross process?

9. What is a key light?

10. Is it necessary to have a portfolio?

Appendix

GLOSSARY

A

Accentuate: To emphasize or to make prominent.

Adhesive: A sticky material used to attach items together.

Adverse reaction: Creating unfavorable or harmful results.

Age Spots: A discoloration on the surface of the skin caused by the aging process.

Aging: The process of growing old.

Airbrush: A small hand-held spray gun used for spraying paint or make-up onto a subject.

99% Alcohol: Colorless volatile inflammable liquid used to thin make-up.

Allergy: An adverse reaction to certain substances.

Analyze: To examine in detail.

Angle: To give a specific point of view.

Application: The act of applying or putting to use.

Arch: Highest point of the eye brow.

Assimilate: Cause to resemble.

B

Back light: Illuminates everything behind the subject.

Base: Make-up product used to even out skin tone.

Base Color: A flesh-tone make-up.

Base Match: A flesh-tone make-up that matches the model perfectly.

Blend: Equal transition from one shade to another.

Brow Bone: The ridge of prominence over the eye.

C

Camouflage: To disguise.

Characteristic: Inherent trait.

Cheek Bone: Bone below the eye, also known as the zygomatic arch.

Cheek Color: A make-up product that is applied to the center of the cheekbone. It comes in powder and cream formulas.

Colored Pencils: Artist pencils in a variety of colors.

Compressor: A machine used for compressing air for use with an airbrush.

Concave: Inverted arch.

Concealer: A make-up product used to color correct.

Concentration: Strength or density.

Contaminate: To render impure by contact or mixture, pollute, taint.

Continuity: To be continuous, as in no visible breaks in continuing scenes.

Contour: To make or form the contour or outline of.

Corners of the Mouth: Where the upper and lower lips meet at the outside edge.

Coverage: A term used to describe how translucent or how opaque a foundation is. A foundation that is translucent has sheer coverage. A foundation that is opaque has full coverage.

Crease: A deep line or wrinkle in the face.

Cream: An emulsified cosmetic.

Cupid's Bow: The center area of the upper lip that appears to have two peaks and a valley.

Curvature: The roundness of an object.

Cylinder: A geometric shape that has a curved surface.

D

Damp: Slightly wet.

Depression: A hollow on a surface.

Depth: Deepness, a measurement from the top down.

Desensitize: To numb slightly.

Discoloration: To alter or mar the hue of a color.

Distinguishing: Recognize, stands out.

Drag: To pull along with effort.

Drop Shadow: Used to create the illusion of a thick lower lash line/to balance a heavy upper eye treatment.

Dual Finish: A flesh color make-up that is a combination of a cream and powder.

E

Elasticity: The ability to stretch.

Exfoliation: To remove dead skin scales by means of a slightly abrasive skin-care product.

Eye Brow: The arch or ridge forming the upper part of the orbit of the eye, or the fringe of hair growing above it.

Eye Fold: The space between the upper lid line and under the brow. Folds can either be one of or in combination with any of the following: slight fold, flat eye, recessed eye, heavy fold, Asian slight fold, and Asian heavy fold.

Eye Lashes: Hairs that grow from the upper and lower eye lids.

Eye Liner: Make-up product that is used to shape, add definition to and enhance the eye. Liquid, pencil and eye shadow may all be used as eye liners.

Eye Shadow: Colored powder or cream make-up product used to enhance, highlight, or shade the eyes.

Eye Pencil: Make-up pencil that is used to shape, define and enhance the eyes.

Eye Pouch: The baggy protrusion located under the eye.

F

Face Chart: A chart used to design or maintain the look of a character.

Fatty Tissue: Area above the eye that begins to hang down as we age.

Feathered: Blended carefully into the skin.

Fill Light: This light fills in areas that the key light leaves in shadow.

Fossa: A depression in the skull.

Frontal Bone: The forehead bone.

Foundation: Make-up product that evens out the skin, toning down slight imperfections and flaws. Foundation is available in a variety of formulations, has different amounts of coverage from sheer to full coverage and finishes (matte to soft sheen.)

G

Gaunt: Very lean or haggard.

Gravity: Force that draws objects to the earth's center.

Gray Scale: Means to measure light to dark.

H

Hair Light: Also known as a Rim Light. Is placed above and slightly behind the subject.

Hard Edge: The sharp division between highlight and shadow is known as a hard edge.

Highlight: Term used in make-up and art that means to bring light to an area. Highlights pull details forward. In make-up, highlights are used to enhance, soften and correct the negative influences of shadows on the face.

Head-shot: An 8x10 professional photograph of an actor.

Horizontal: Parallel to the plane of the horizon.

I

Intricate: Fine detail.

Illusion: The ability to make something appear to be what it is not.

Intrinsic: Inherent; essential; innate; belonging entirely to the thing in itself.

Iridescent: Reflects light and has shine.

J

Jowl: Fleshy part of the jaw line.

K

Key Light: The main source of illumination on set.

L

Labial Roll: The natural highlight that surrounds the edge of the lips.

Liberal: To use a lot of something.

Lip Gloss: A make-up product for the lips that is thicker than lipstick and imparts a high shine. Can be worn alone, over lip liner, or over lip liner and lipstick.

Lip Line: The defined edge that surrounds the upper and lower lip.

Lip Liner: A make-up pencil that is used to shape, define and color lips.

Lipstick: A make-up product that is used to color the lips. Comes in a variety of finishes, such as matte or cream.

Liquid: A substance that moves freely and easily.

M

Male Corrective: A make-up technique done on men.

Mascara: An eye make-up product that colors, lengthens and thickens the eyelashes. It is available in a variety of colors and formulations.

Matte: Not shiny, does not reflect light.

Mature: Older

Muted: Opposite of intense.

N

Nasolabial Fold: The crease that runs from above the nostril down to the corner of the mouth.

Neutralize: To cancel out.

Nostrils: The two openings of the nose.

Nozzle: The tip of the airbrush.

O

Obscure: Not clear or distinct to any sense.

Olive: A yellow green colored undertone.

Opaque: Impossible to see through.

Orbital Rim: Belonging to the eye socket.

P

Palette: A metal, wax or acrylic piece used as a holding area for make-up.

Palette Knife: Artist knife used to sculpt wax and to scoop make-up from containers.

Pigmented Powder: Talc and pigment mixed together to form a translucent powder.

Pliable: Able to bend or move easily.

Portfolio: A collection of the artist's work.

Powder: Talc that is used for setting make-up and decreasing shine.

Powder Puff: A velour pad used to hold powder.

Precautions: Care taken beforehand to avoid risk or injury.

Primary Colors: Red, blue and yellow.

Pigment: Coloring matter usually in powder form mixed with oils, water, etc., to create a colored cosmetic. In foundation, pigment is the element of the foundations that provide shade/color and coverage.
Powder: A make-up product that comes in loose and pressed forms. Powder is used to set make-up, absorb oil, and soften make up applications. Powder comes in a variety of natural shades to match and complement all skin tones.

R

Random: Without method or conscious choice.

Ruddy: A reddish undertone.

S

Sanitation: The maintenance of sanitary conditions.

Secondary Color: Created by mixing two primary colors together.

Set Bag: A bag used to carry items needed on set to do touch-ups.

Severe: Very harsh.

Shadow: To darken or cast by an object between a light source and a subject.

Shade: The value of lightness/darkness of a color, and one of the necessary elements in matching skin tones when choosing foundation.

Shadow: A term used in both make-up and art that refers to an area that receives less light- therefore being in shade. Shadow "pushes" details back, creating depth. In make-up, shadows are used to contour and reduce the negative effects of highlighted areas on the face.

Sheer: Translucent:

Shine: A highly reflective spot or area caused by moisture or perspiration.

Skin Tone: A combination of shade and undertone used to determine the foundation color for the model's skin.

Slip: A term used in cosmetics to describe the consistency of a liquid or cream product. The more slip a product has, the creamier it feels.

Slurry: Created by water mixed with a cake make-up product, such as eye liner.

Smearing: To spread with force.

Soft Edge: The gradation between highlight and shadow.

SPF: Sun Protection Factor. Means to measure the amount of protection in a sunscreen.

Sunscreen: A lotion or cream product that is applied to the skin to protect it from damage caused by the sun.

Symmetry: Perfect balance between two sides.

T

Talc: A hydrous magnesium silicate.

Taper: To diminish as it moves away.

Tattoo: Permanent art on the skin.

Temporal Fossa: Depression on each side of the forehead.

Tear Duct: The duct in the innermost corner of the eye where tears are formed

Tertiary Color: Created when mixing a secondary color with a primary color.

Test Make-up: A make-up done prior to the shoot date to establish the look.

Texture: The representation of the surface structure of an object.

Thick: Firm in consistency.

Three Dimensional: Height, Depth and Width.

Translucent: Sheer, allowing light to pass through.

Tweeze: To remove single hairs one at a time from the eye brows.

Tweezers: A small tool used for grabbing small items.

Two Dimensional: Height and width, no depth.

U

Undertone: The intrinsic color of the skin ranging from ruddy to olive. Undertone is the second element that is necessary to understand, when selecting a foundation color that enhances/matches the skin.

Upper Lid: Tissue that covers the eye where the upper eye lashes are located.

V

Vehicle: A means of transporting pigment.
In foundation or base, the pigment is mixed with a vehicle of oil/water to create the foundation. Vehicle is the element of foundation that gives it slip.

Veins: Any of the tubes conveying blood to the heart

Vertical: At right angle to the plane of horizontal.

W

Wardrobe: Clothing worn by an actor in films.

Wedge: Shape that progressively increases at a right angle.

White Sponge: A foam sponge used to apply make-up to a performer.

Wrinkles: Lines and creases in the face caused by aging.

Z

Zinc Oxide: White pigment.

Zygomatic Arch: The cheek bone.

INDEX

Make-Up Designory is a California state-licensed, private postsecondary institution whose primary objective is to provide training in fashion, film and television make-up artistry, and other related arts. Vocational training is provided to those individuals seeking employment in the entertainment and fashion industries, and those in need of continuing education in their chosen field of make-up artistry, fashion styling, or hairstyling. Make-Up Designory is dedicated to providing education in the craft of make-up artistry and related fields that are specific to the needs of both the novice and the experienced artist.

Make-Up Designory was formed in 1997 by a group of school administrators and instructors in order to bring excellence to make-up education. The school's founding philosophy was to offer unparalleled education, make the students first, and create an institution for learning which the make-up community, as a whole, could be proud of. Make-Up Designory became a nationally accredited school in February 2003, earning a "School of Distinction" Award from the Accrediting Commission of Career Schools and Colleges of Technology.

The Instructors are state-licensed, qualified teachers who bring years of practical working experience to the classroom. Each professional brings real world experience and talent along with the prepared program of instruction. The 11,000 foot campus includes nine fully-equipped modern classrooms, a video/photography studio, an effective resource and research library, a student lounge, a make-up supply store, and all the administrative services necessary for a thorough and practical education.

Classes are offered year-round, with day and night schedules available.
Offered subjects are:
Beauty Make-up Artistry Course
Character Make-up Artistry Course
Special Make-up Effects Course
Studio Hairstyling Course
Fashion Styling Program
Journeyman Make-up Artistry Program
Master Make-up Artistry Program

If you would like more information, or to request a school catalog:

Call:
818-729-9420

Write:
Make-up Designory
129 S. San Fernando Blvd.
Burbank, CA. 91502

Surf the net:
www.makeupschool.com
www.makeupdesignory.com
www.mud.edu

For information regarding
Make-up Designory products:
Call the mudshop:
818-557-7619
Or shop online at:
www.mudshop.com